THE EIGHTH AMENDMENT

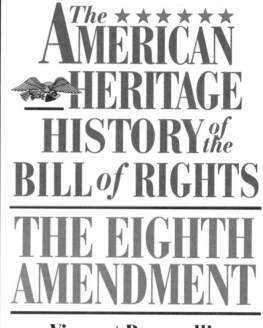

The ★★★★★★★ AMERICAN HERITAGE HISTORY of the BILL of RIGHTS

THE EIGHTH AMENDMENT

Vincent Buranelli

Introduction by
WARREN E. BURGER
Chief Justice of the United States
1969–1986

Silver Burdett Press

To Nan

Cover: A prison fence and guard tower. The Eighth Amendment clause about "cruel and unusual punishments" is usually applied in judging fairness of sentences, but it is also involved in the debate that surrounds two currently controversial and complicated issues—the death penalty and insanity pleas.

CONSULTANTS:

Elizabeth Blackmar
Assistant Professor of History
Columbia College
New York, New York

Robert M. Goldberg
Consultant to Social Studies
  Department (formerly
  Department Chair)
Oceanside Middle School
Oceanside, New York

Michael H. Reggio
Law-Related Education
  Coordinator
Oklahoma Bar Association
Oklahoma City, Oklahoma

Text and Cover Design: Circa 86, Inc.

Library of Congress Cataloging-in-Publication Data

Buranelli, Vincent.
  The Eighth Amendment/by Vincent Buranelli: with an introduction
by Warren E. Burger.
    p. cm.—(The American Heritage history of the Bill of
Rights)
  Includes bibliographical references and indexes.
  Summary: Studies the historical origins of provisions of the Eighth Amendment, which guards
against excessive bail and fines and cruel and unusual punishments.
    1. United States—Constitutional law—Amendments—8th—History—
Juvenile literature. 2. Bail—United States—History—Juvenile literature. 3. Fines (Penalties)—United
States—History—Juvenile literature. 4. Punishment—United States—History—Juvenile literature. [1.
United States—Constitutional law—Amendments—8th—History. 2. Bail—History. 3. Fines
(Penalties)—History. 4. Punishment—History.] I. Title. II. Series.
KF4558 8th. B87 1991
345. 73'056—dc20
[347.30556]   90-48850
                                                                                    CIP
                                                                                    AC

Manufactured in the United States of America.

ISBN 0-382-24187-8 [lib. bdg.]
10 9 8 7 6 5 4 3 2 1

ISBN 0-382-24199-1 [pbk.]
10 9 8 7 6 5 4 3 2 1

$\mathscr{C}$ONTENTS

$\mathcal{I}$NTRODUCTION

WARREN E. BURGER
Chief Justice of the United States, 1969–1986

The Eighth Amendment protects persons accused of crimes from being charged excessive bail while they are awaiting or undergoing trial. If they are convicted of a crime, it also protects them from excessive fines or other "cruel and unusual punishments." These protections are essential safeguards of individual liberty.

Concepts of liberty—the values liberty protects—inspired the Framers of our Constitution and the Bill of Rights to some of their most impassioned eloquence. "Liberty, the greatest of earthly possessions—give us that precious jewel, and you may take everything else," declaimed Patrick Henry. Those toilers in the "vineyard of liberty" sensed the historic nature of their mission, and their foresight accounts for the survival of the Bill of Rights.

Though most of us will not be defendants in criminal cases, we all have an interest in Eighth Amendment rights. Law-abiding citizens have legitimate concerns about the rules under which potentially dangerous criminals are released on bail pending trial. We must balance public safety—the personal liberty of the larger population—against that of the individual defendant. The Eighth Amendment also enters into discussions of the appropriate punishment for white-collar crime, of corporal punishment in schools, and of the death penalty and insanity plea. And it is a safeguard against bias in the sentencing of convicted criminals.

The long-term success of the system of ordered liberty set up by our Constitution was by no means foreordained. The bicentennial of the Bill of Rights provides an opportunity to reflect on the significance of the freedoms we enjoy and to commit ourselves to exercise the civic responsibilities required to sustain our constitutional system. The Constitution, including its first ten amendments, the Bill of Rights, has survived two centuries because of its unprecedented philosophical premise: that it derives its power from the people. It is not a grant from the government to the people. In 1787 the masters—the people—were saying to their government—their servant—that certain rights are inherent, natural rights and that they belong to the people, who had those rights before any governments existed. The function of government, they said, was to protect these rights.

The Bill of Rights also owes its continued vitality to the fact that it was drafted by experienced, practical politicians. It was a product of the Framers' essential mistrust of the frailties of human nature. This led them to develop the idea of the separation of powers and to make the Bill of Rights part of the permanent Constitution.

Moreover, the document was designed to be flexible, and the role of providing that flexibility through interpretation has fallen to the judiciary. Indeed, the first commander in chief, George Washington, gave the Supreme Court its moral marching orders two centuries ago when he said, "the administration of justice is the firmest pillar of government." The principle of judicial review as a check on government has perhaps nowhere been more significant than in the protection of individual liberties. It has been my privilege, along with my colleagues on the Court, to ensure the continued vitality of our Bill of Rights. As John Marshall asked, long before he became chief justice, "To what quarter will you look for a protection from an infringement on the Constitution, if you will not give the power to the judiciary?"

But the preservation of the Bill of Rights is not the sole responsibility of the judiciary. Rather, judges, legislatures, and presidents are partners with every American; liberty is the responsibility of every public officer and every citizen. In this spirit all Americans should become acquainted with the principles and history of this most remarkable document. Its bicentennial should not be simply a celebration but the beginning of an ongoing process. Americans must—by their conduct—guarantee that it continues to protect the sacred rights of our uniquely multicultural population. We must not fail to exercise our rights to vote, to participate in government and community activities, and to implement the principles of liberty, tolerance, opportunity, and justice for all.

THE AMERICAN HERITAGE
HISTORY OF THE BILL OF RIGHTS

THE FIRST AMENDMENT
by Philip A. Klinkner

THE SECOND AMENDMENT
by Joan C. Hawxhurst

THE THIRD AMENDMENT
by Burnham Holmes

THE FOURTH AMENDMENT
by Paula A. Franklin

THE FIFTH AMENDMENT
by Burnham Holmes

THE SIXTH AMENDMENT
by Eden Force

THE SEVENTH AMENDMENT
by Lila E. Summer

THE EIGHTH AMENDMENT
by Vincent Buranelli

THE NINTH AMENDMENT
by Philip A. Klinkner

THE TENTH AMENDMENT
by Judith Adams

The Bill of Rights

AMENDMENT 1*
Article Congress shall make no law respecting an establishment of religion, or prohibiting the free exercise thereof; or abridging the freedom of speech, or of the press; or the right of the people peaceably to assemble, and to petition the Government for a redress of grievances.

AMENDMENT 2
Article A well regulated Militia, being necessary to the security of a free State, the right of the people to keep and bear Arms, shall not be infringed.

AMENDMENT 3
Article No Soldier shall, in time of peace be quartered in any house, without the consent of the Owner, nor in time of war, but in a manner to be prescribed by law.

AMENDMENT 4
Article The right of the people to be secure in their persons, houses, papers, and effects, against unreasonable searches and seizures, shall not be violated, and no Warrants shall issue, but upon probable cause, supported by Oath or affirmation, and particularly describing the place to be searched, and the persons or things to be seized.

AMENDMENT 5
Article No person shall be held to answer for a capital, or otherwise infamous crime, unless on a presentment or indictment of a Grand Jury, except in cases arising in the land or naval forces, or in the Militia, when in actual service in time of War or public danger; nor shall any person be subject for the same offence to be twice put in jeopardy of life or limb; nor shall be compelled in any criminal case to be a witness against himself, nor be deprived of life, liberty, or property, without due process of law; nor shall private property be taken for public use without just compensation.

AMENDMENT 6
Article In all criminal prosecutions, the accused shall enjoy the right to a speedy and public trial, by an impartial jury of the State and district wherein the crime shall have been committed, which district shall have been previously ascertained by law, and to be informed of the nature and cause of the accusation; to be confronted with the witnesses against him; to have compulsory process for obtaining Witnesses in his favor, and to have the assistance of counsel for his defence.

AMENDMENT 7
Article In Suits at common law, where the value in controversy shall exceed twenty dollars, the right of trial by jury shall be preserved, and no fact tried by a jury, shall be otherwise reexamined in any Court of the United States, than according to the rules of the common law.

AMENDMENT 8
Article Excessive bail shall not be required, nor excessive fines imposed, nor cruel and unusual punishments inflicted.

AMENDMENT 9
Article The enumeration in the Constitution, of certain rights, shall not be construed to deny or disparage others retained by the people.

AMENDMENT 10
Article The powers not delegated to the United States by the Constitution, nor prohibited by it to the States, are reserved to the States respectively, or to the people.

*Note that each of the first ten amendments to the original Constitution is called an "Article." None of these amendments had actual numbers at the time of their ratification.

THE HISTORY OF THE
BILL OF RIGHTS

1770s–1790s

1774 Quartering Act
1775 Revolutionary War begins
1776 Declaration of Independence is signed.
1783 Revolutionary War ends.
1787 Constitutional Convention writes the U.S. Constitution.
1788 U.S. Constitution is ratified by most states.
1789 Congress proposes the Bill of Rights
1791 The Bill of Rights is ratified by the states.
1792 Militia Act

1800s–1820s

1803 *Marbury* v. *Madison*. Supreme Court declares that it has the power of judicial review and exercises it. This is the first case in which the Court holds a law of Congress unconstitutional.
1807 Trial of Aaron Burr. Ruling that juries may have knowledge of a case so long as they have not yet formed an opinion.
1813 Kentucky becomes the first state to outlaw concealed weapons.
1824 *Gibbons* v. *Ogden*. Supreme Court defines Congress's power to regulate commerce, including trade between states and within states if that commerce affects other states.

1830s–1870s

1833 *Barron* v. *Baltimore.* Supreme Court rules that Bill of Rights applies only to actions of the federal government, not to the states and local governments.

1851 *Cooley* v. *Board of Wardens of the Port of Philadelphia.* Supreme Court rules that states can apply their own rules to some foreign and interstate commerce if their rules are of a local nature—unless or until Congress makes rules for particular situations.

1857 *Dred Scott* v. *Sandford.* Supreme Court denies that African Americans are citizens even if they happen to live in a "free state."

1862 Militia Act

1865 Thirteenth Amendment is ratified. Slavery is not allowed in the United States.

1868 Fourteenth Amendment is ratified. All people born or naturalized in the United States are citizens. Their privileges and immunities are protected, as are their life, liberty, and property according to due process. They have equal protection of the laws.

1873 *Slaughterhouse* cases. Supreme Court rules that the Fourteenth Amendment does not limit state power to make laws dealing with economic matters. Court mentions the unenumerated right to political participation.

1876 *United States* v. *Cruikshank.* Supreme Court rules that the right to bear arms for a lawful purpose is not an absolute right granted by the Constitution. States can limit this right and make their own gun-control laws.

1880s–1920s

1884 *Hurtado* v. *California.* Supreme Court rules that the right to a grand jury indictment doesn't apply to the states.

1896 *Plessy* v. *Ferguson.* Supreme Court upholds a state law based on "separate but equal" facilities for different races.

1903 Militia Act creates National Guard.

1905 *Lochner* v. *New York.* Supreme Court strikes down a state law regulating maximum work hours.

1914 *Weeks* v. *United States.* Supreme Court establishes that illegally obtained evidence, obtained by unreasonable search and seizure, cannot be used in federal trials.

1918 *Hammer* v. *Dagenhart.* Supreme Court declares unconstitutional a federal law prohibiting the shipment between states of goods made by young children.

1923 *Meyer* v. *Nebraska.* Supreme Court rules that a law banning teaching of foreign languages or teaching in languages other than English is unconstitutional. Court says that certain areas of people's private lives are protected from government interference.

1925 *Carroll* v. *United States.* Supreme Court allows searches of automobiles without a search warrant under some circumstances.

1925 *Gitlow* v. *New York.* Supreme Court rules that freedom of speech and freedom of the press are protected from state actions by the Fourteenth Amendment.

1930s

1931 *Near* v. *Minnesota*. Supreme Court rules that liberty of the press and of speech are safeguarded from state action.

1931 *Stromberg* v. *California*. Supreme Court extends concept of freedom of speech to symbolic actions such as displaying a flag.

1932 *Powell* v. *Alabama* (*First Scottsboro* case). Supreme Court rules that poor defendants have a right to an appointed lawyer when tried for crimes that may result in the death penalty.

1934 National Firearms Act becomes the first federal law to restrict the keeping and bearing of arms.

1935 *Norris* v. *Alabama* (*Second Scottsboro* case). Supreme Court reverses the conviction of an African American because of the long continued excluding of African Americans from jury service in the trial area.

1937 *Palko* v. *Connecticut*. Supreme Court refuses to require states to protect people under the double jeopardy clause of the Bill of Rights. But the case leads to future application of individual rights in the Bill of Rights to the states on a case-by-case basis.

1937 *DeJonge* v. *Oregon*. Supreme Court rules that freedom of assembly and petition are protected against state laws.

1939 *United States* v. *Miller*. Supreme Court rules that National Firearms Act of 1934 does not violate Second Amendment.

1940s–1950s

1940 *Cantwell* v. *Connecticut*. Supreme Court rules that free exercise of religion is protected against state laws.

1943 *Barnette* v. *West Virginia State Board of Education*. Supreme Court rules that flag salute laws are unconstitutional.

1946 *Theil* v. *Pacific Railroad*. Juries must be a cross section of the community, excluding no group based on religion, race, sex, or economic status.

1947 *Everson* v. *Board of Education*. Supreme Court rules that government attempts to impose religious practices, the establishment of religion, is forbidden to the states.

1948 *In re Oliver*. Supreme Court rules that defendants have a right to public trial in nonfederal trials.

1949 *Wolf* v. *California*. Supreme Court rules that freedom from unreasonable searches and seizures also applies to states.

1954 *Brown* v. *Board of Education of Topeka*. Supreme Court holds that segregation on the basis of race (in public education) denies equal protection of the laws.

1958 *NAACP* v. *Alabama*. Supreme Court rules that the privacy of membership lists in an organization is part of the right to freedom of assembly and association.

1960s

1961 *Mapp* v. *Ohio.* Supreme Court rules that illegally obtained evidence must not be allowed in state criminal trials.

1962 *Engel* v. *Vitale.* Supreme Court strikes down state-sponsored school prayer, saying it is no business of government to compose official prayers as part of a religious program carried on by the government.

1963 *Gideon* v. *Wainwright.* Supreme Court rules that the right of people accused of serious crimes to be represented by an appointed counsel applies to state criminal trials.

1964 Civil Rights Act is passed.

1964 *Malloy* v. *Hogan.* Supreme Court rules that the right to protection against forced self-incrimination applies to state trials.

1965 *Griswold* v. *Connecticut.* Supreme Court rules that there is a right to privacy in marriage and declares unconstitutional a state law banning the use of or the giving of information about birth control.

1965 *Pointer* v. *Texas.* Supreme Court rules that the right to confront witnesses against an accused person applies to state trials.

1966 *Parker* v. *Gladden.* Supreme Court ruling is interpreted to mean that the right to an impartial jury is applied to the states.

1966 *Miranda* v. *Arizona.* Supreme Court extends the protection against forced self-incrimination. Police have to inform people in custody of their rights before questioning them.

1967 *Katz* v. *United States.* Supreme Court rules that people's right to be free of unreasonable searches includes protection against electronic surveillance.

1967 *Washington* v. *Texas.* Supreme Court rules that accused people have the right to have witnesses in their favor brought into court.

1967 *In re Gault.* Supreme Court rules that juvenile proceedings that might lead to the young person's being sent to a state institution must follow due process and fair treatment. These include the rights against forced self-incrimination, to counsel, to confront witnesses.

1967 *Klopfer* v. *North Carolina.* Supreme Court rules that the right to a speedy trial applies to state trials.

1968 *Duncan* v. *Louisiana.* Supreme Court rules that the right to a jury trial in criminal cases applies to state trials.

1969 *Benton* v. *Maryland.* Supreme Court rules that the protection against double jeopardy applies to the states.

1969 *Brandenburg* v. *Ohio.* Supreme Court rules that speech calling for the use of force or crime can only be prohibited if it is directed to bringing about immediate lawless action and is likely to bring about such action.

1970s–1990s

1970 *Williams* v. *Florida.* Juries in cases that do not lead to the possibility of the death penalty may consist of six jurors rather than twelve.

1971 *Pentagon Papers* case. Freedom of the press is protected by forbidding prior restraint.

1971 *Duke Power Co.* v. *Carolina Environmental Study Group, Inc.* Supreme Court upholds state law limiting liability of federally licensed power companies in the event of a nuclear accident.

1972 *Furman* v. *Georgia.* Supreme Court rules that the death penalty (as it was then decided upon) is cruel and unusual punishment and therefore unconstitutional.

1972 *Argersinger* v. *Hamlin.* Supreme Court rules that right to counsel applies to all criminal cases that might involve a jail term.

1973 *Roe* v. *Wade.* Supreme Court declares that the right to privacy protects a woman's right to end pregnancy by abortion under specified circumstances.

1976 *Gregg* v. *Georgia.* Supreme Court rules that the death penalty is to be allowed if it is decided upon in a consistent and reasonable way, if the sentencing follows strict guidelines, and if the penalty is not required for certain crimes.

1976 *National League of Cities* v. *Usery.* Supreme Court holds that the Tenth Amendment prevents Congress from making federal minimum wage and overtime rules apply to state and city workers.

1981 *Quilici* v. *Village of Morton Grove.* U.S. district court upholds a local ban on sale and possession of handguns.

1985 *Garcia* v. *San Antonio Metropolitan Transit Authority.* Supreme Court rules that Congress can make laws dealing with wages and hour rules applied to city-owned transportation systems.

1989 *Webster* v. *Reproductive Health Services.* Supreme Court holds that a state may prohibit all use of public facilities and publicly employed staff in abortions.

1989 *Johnson* v. *Texas.* Supreme Court rules that flag burning is protected and is a form of "symbolic speech."

1990 *Cruzan* v. *Missouri Department of Health.* Supreme Court recognizes for the first time a very sick person's right to die without being forced to undergo unwanted medical treatment and a person's right to a living will.

1990 *Noriega–CNN* case. Supreme Court upholds lower federal court's decision to allow temporary prior restraint thus limiting the First Amendment right of freedom of the press.

The Birth of the Bill of Rights

"We hold these truths to be self-evident, that all men are created equal, that they are endowed by their Creator with certain unalienable Rights, that among these are Life, Liberty, and the pursuit of Happiness."

THE DECLARATION OF INDEPENDENCE (1776)

A brave Chinese student standing in front of a line of tanks, Eastern Europeans marching against the secret police, happy crowds dancing on top of the Berlin Wall—these were recent scenes of people trying to gain their freedom or celebrating it. The scenes and the events that sparked them will live on in history. They also show the lasting gift that is our Bill of Rights. The freedoms guaranteed by the Bill of Rights have guided and inspired millions of people all over the world in their struggle for freedom.

The Colonies Gain Their Freedom

Like many countries today, the United States fought to gain freedom and democracy for itself. The American colonies had a revolution from 1775 to 1783 to free themselves from British rule.

The colonists fought to free themselves because they believed that the British had violated, or gone against, their rights. The colonists held what some considered the extreme idea that all

James Madison is known as both the "Father of the Constitution" and the "Father of the Bill of Rights." In 1789 he proposed to Congress the amendments that became the Bill of Rights. Madison served two terms as president of the United States from 1809 to 1817.

The Raising of the Liberty Pole by John McRae. In 1776, American colonists hoisted liberty poles as symbols of liberty and freedom from British rule. At the top they usually placed a liberty cap. Such caps resembled the caps given to slaves in ancient Rome when they were freed.

persons are born with certain rights. They believed that these rights could not be taken away, even by the government. The importance our nation gave to individual rights can be seen in the Declaration of Independence. The Declaration, written by Thomas Jefferson in 1776, states:

> We hold these truths to be self-evident, that all men are created equal, that they are endowed by their Creator with certain unalienable Rights, that among these are Life, Liberty, and the pursuit of Happiness.

The United States won its independence from Britain in 1783. But with freedom came the difficult job of forming a government. The Americans wanted a government that was strong enough to keep peace and prosperity, but not so strong that it might take away the rights for which the Revolution had been fought. The Articles of Confederation was the country's first written plan of government.

The Articles of Confederation, becoming law in 1781, created a weak national government. The defects in the Articles soon became clear to many Americans. Because the United States did not have a strong national government, its economy suffered. Under the Articles, Congress did not have the power to tax. It had to ask the states for money or borrow it. There was no separate president or court system. Nine of the states had to agree before Congress's bills became law. In 1786 economic problems caused farmers in Massachusetts to revolt. The national government was almost powerless to stop the revolt. It was also unable to build an army or navy strong enough to protect the United States's borders and its ships on the high seas.

The Constitution Is Drawn Up

The nation's problems had to be solved. So, in February 1787, the Continental Congress asked the states to send delegates to a convention to discuss ways of improving the Articles. That May, fifty-five delegates, from every state except Rhode Island, met in Philadelphia. The group included some of the country's most famous leaders: George Washington, hero of the Revolution; Benjamin Franklin, publisher, inventor, and diplomat; and James Madison, a leading critic of the Articles. Madison would soon become the guiding force behind the Constitutional Convention.

After a long, hot summer of debate the delegates finally drew up the document that became the U.S. Constitution. It set up a strong central government. But it also divided power between three branches of the federal government. These three branches were the executive branch (the presidency), the legislative branch (Congress), and the judicial branch (the courts). Each was given one part of the government's power. This division was to make sure that no single branch became so powerful that it could violate the people's rights.

The legislative branch (made up of the House of Representatives and the Senate) would have the power to pass laws, raise taxes and spend money, regulate the national economy, and declare war. The executive branch was given the power to carry out the laws, run foreign affairs, and command the military.

The Signing of the Constitution painted by Thomas Rossiter. The Constitutional Convention met in Philadelphia from May into September 1787. The proposed Constitution contained protection for some individual rights such as protection against *ex post facto* laws and bills of attainder. When the Constitution was ratified by the required number of states in 1788, however, it did not have a bill of rights.

The role of the judicial branch in this plan was less clear. The Constitution said that the judicial branch would have "judicial power." However, it was unclear exactly what this power was. Over the years "judicial power" has come to mean "judicial review." The power of judicial review allows the federal courts to reject laws passed by Congress or the state legislatures that they believe violate the Constitution.

Judicial review helps protect our rights. It allows federal courts to reject laws that violate the Constitution's guarantees of individual rights. Because of this power, James Madison believed that the courts would be an "impenetrable bulwark," an unbreakable wall, against any attempt by government to take away these rights.

The Constitution did more than divide the power of the federal government among the three branches. It also divided power between the states and the federal government. This division of power is known as *federalism.* Federalism means that the federal

government has control over certain areas. These include regulating the national economy and running foreign and military affairs. The states have control over most other areas. For example, they regulate their economies and make most other laws. Once again, the Framers (writers) of the Constitution hoped that the division of powers would keep both the states and the federal government from becoming too strong and possibly violating individual rights.

The new Constitution did *not,* however, contain a bill of rights. Such a bill would list the people's rights and would forbid the government from interfering with them. The only discussion of the topic came late in the convention. At that time, George Mason of Virginia called for a bill of rights. A Connecticut delegate, Roger Sherman, disagreed. He claimed that a bill of rights was not needed. In his view, the Constitution did not take away any of the rights in the bills of rights in the state constitutions. These had been put in place during the Revolution. The other delegates agreed with Roger Sherman. Mason's proposal was voted down by all.

Yet the Constitution was not without guarantees of individual rights. One of these rights was the protection of *habeas corpus.* This is a legal term that refers to the right of someone who has been arrested to be brought into court and formally charged with a crime. Another right forbade *ex post facto* laws. These are laws that outlaw actions that took place before the passage of the laws. Other parts of the Constitution forbade bills of attainder (laws pronouncing a person guilty of a crime without trial), required jury trials, restricted convictions for treason, and guaranteed a republican form of government. That is a government in which political power rests with citizens who vote for elected officials and representatives responsible to the voters. The Constitution also forbade making public officials pass any "religious test." This meant that religious requirements could not be forced on public officials.

The Debate Over the New Constitution

Once it was written, the Constitution had to be ratified, or approved, by nine of the states before it could go into effect. The new

Constitution created much controversy. Heated battles raged in many states over whether or not to approve the document. One of the main arguments used by those who opposed the Constitution (the Anti-Federalists) was that the Constitution made the federal government too strong. They feared that it might violate the rights of the people just as the British government had. Although he had helped write the Constitution, Anti-Federalist George Mason opposed it for this reason. He claimed that he would sooner chop off his right hand than put it to the Constitution as it then stood.

To correct what they viewed as flaws in the Constitution, the Anti-Federalists insisted that it have a bill of rights. The fiery orator of the Revolution, Patrick Henry, another Anti-Federalist, exclaimed, "Liberty, the greatest of all earthly blessings—give us that precious jewel, and you may take every thing else!"

Although he was not an Anti-Federalist, Thomas Jefferson also believed that a bill of rights was needed. He wrote a letter to James Madison, a wavering Federalist, in which he said: "A bill of rights is what the people are entitled to against every government on earth."

Supporters of the Constitution (the Federalists) argued that it did not need a bill of rights. One reason they stated, similar to that given at the Philadelphia convention, was that most state constitutions had a bill of rights. Nothing in the Constitution would limit or abolish these rights. In 1788 James Madison wrote that he thought a bill of rights would provide only weak "parchment barriers" against attempts by government to take away individual rights. He believed that history had shown that a bill of rights was ineffective on "those occasions when its control [was] needed most."

The views of the Anti-Federalists seem to have had more support than did those of the Federalists. The Federalists came to realize that without a bill of rights, the states might not approve the new Constitution. To ensure ratification, the Federalists therefore agreed to support adding a bill of rights to the Constitution.

With this compromise, eleven of the thirteen states ratified the Constitution by July 1788. The new government of the United States was born. The two remaining states, North Carolina and

Rhode Island, in time accepted the new Constitution. North Carolina approved it in November 1789 and Rhode Island in May 1790.

James Madison Calls for a Bill of Rights

On April 30, 1789, George Washington took the oath of office as president. The new government was launched. One of its first jobs was to amend, or change, the Constitution to include a bill of rights. This is what many of the states had called for during the ratification process. Leading this effort in the new Congress was James Madison. He was a strong supporter of individual rights. As a member of the Virginia legislature, he had helped frame the Virginia Declaration of Rights. He had also fought for religious liberty.

Madison, however, had at first opposed including a bill of rights. But his views had changed. He feared that the Constitution would not be ratified by enough states to become law unless the Federalists offered to include a bill of rights. Madison also knew that many people were afraid of the new government. He feared they might oppose its actions or attempt to undo it. He said a bill of rights "will kill the opposition everywhere, and by putting an end to disaffection to [discontent with] the Government itself, enable the administration to venture on measures not otherwise safe."

On June 8, 1789, the thirty-eight-year-old Madison rose to speak in the House of Representatives. He called for several changes to the Constitution that contained the basis of our present Bill of Rights. Despite his powerful words, Madison's speech did not excite his listeners. Most Federalists in Congress opposed a bill of rights. Others believed that the new Constitution should be given more time to operate before Congress considered making any changes. Many Anti-Federalists wanted a new constitutional convention. There, they hoped to greatly limit the powers of the federal government. These Anti-Federalists thought that adding a bill of rights to the Constitution would prevent their movement for a new convention.

Finally, in August, Madison persuaded the House to consider

his amendments. The House accepted most of them. However, instead of being placed in the relevant sections of the Constitution, as Madison had called for, the House voted to add them as separate amendments. This change—listing the amendments together— made the Bill of Rights the distinct document that it is today.

After approval by the House, the amendments went to the Senate. The Senate dropped what Madison considered the most important part of his plan. This was the protection of freedom of the press, freedom of religious belief, and the right to trial by jury from violation by the states. Protection of these rights from violation by state governments would have to wait until after the Fourteenth Amendment was adopted in 1868.

The House and the Senate at last agreed on ten amendments to protect individual rights. What rights were protected? Here is a partial list:

The First Amendment protects freedom of religion, of speech, of the press, of peaceful assembly, and of petition.

The Second Amendment gives to the states the right to keep a militia (a volunteer, reserve military force) and to the people the right to keep and bear arms.

The Third Amendment prevents the government from keeping troops in private homes during wartime.

The Fourth Amendment protects individuals from unreasonable searches and seizures by the government.

The Fifth Amendment states that the government must get an indictment (an official ruling that a crime has been committed) before someone can be tried for a serious crime. This amendment bans "double jeopardy." This means trying a person twice for the same criminal offense. It also protects people from having to testify against themselves in court.

The Fifth Amendment also says that the government cannot take away a person's "life, liberty, or property, without due process of law." This means that the government must follow fair and just procedures if it takes away a person's "life, liberty, or property." Finally, the Fifth Amendment says that if the government takes property from an individual for public use, it must pay that person an adequate sum of money for the property.

The Sixth Amendment requires that all criminal trials be speedy and public, and decided by a fair jury. The amendment also allows people on trial to know what offense they have been charged with. It also allows them to be present when others testify against them, to call witnesses to their defense, and to have the help of a lawyer.

The Seventh Amendment provides for a jury trial in all cases involving amounts over $20.

The Eighth Amendment forbids unreasonably high bail (money paid to free someone from jail before his or her trial), unreasonably large fines, and cruel and unusual punishments.

The Ninth Amendment says that the rights of the people are not limited only to those listed in the Bill of Rights.

Finally, the Tenth Amendment helps to establish federalism by giving to the states and the people any powers not given to the federal government by the Constitution.

After being approved by the House and the Senate, the amendments were sent to the states for adoption in October 1789. By December 1791, three-fourths of the states had approved the ten amendments we now know as the Bill of Rights. The Bill of Rights had become part of the U.S. Constitution.

How Our Court System Works

Many of the events in this book concern court cases involving the Bill of Rights. To help understand how the U.S. court system works, here is a brief description.

The U.S. federal court system has three levels. At the lowest level are the federal district courts. There are ninety-four district courts, each covering a different area of the United States and its territories. Most cases having to do with the Constitution begin in the district courts.

People who lose their cases in the district courts may then appeal to the next level in the court system, the federal courts of appeals. To appeal means to take your case to a higher court in an attempt to change the lower court's decision. Here, those who are making the appeal try to obtain a different judgment. There are thirteen federal courts of appeals in the United States.

People who lose in the federal courts of appeals may then take their case to the U.S. Supreme Court. It is the highest court in the land. The Supreme Court has the final say in a case. You cannot appeal a Supreme Court decision.

The size of the Supreme Court is set by Congress and has changed over the years. Since 1869 the Supreme Court has been made up of nine justices. One is the chief justice of the United States, and eight are associate justices. The justices are named by the president and confirmed by the Senate.

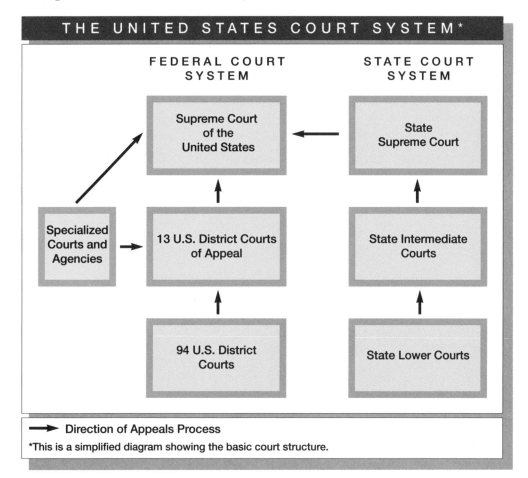

THE UNITED STATES COURT SYSTEM*

FEDERAL COURT SYSTEM

STATE COURT SYSTEM

Supreme Court of the United States

State Supreme Court

Specialized Courts and Agencies

13 U.S. District Courts of Appeal

State Intermediate Courts

94 U.S. District Courts

State Lower Courts

→ Direction of Appeals Process

*This is a simplified diagram showing the basic court structure.

In the Supreme Court, a simple majority of votes is needed to decide a case. If there is a tie, the lower court's decision remains in effect. When the chief justice votes on the majority side, he or she can assign the writing of the opinion to any of the majority justices, including himself or herself. The opinion states the Court's decision and the reasons for it. Who writes the opinion when the chief justice hasn't voted on the majority side? In that case, the longest-serving associate justice who voted for the majority·decision can assign the writing to any of the majority justices, including himself or herself.

What if a justice has voted for the majority decision but doesn't agree with the reasons given in the majority opinion? He or she may write what is called a concurring opinion. That is one which agrees with the Court's decision but for different reasons.

Those justices who disagree with the Court's decision may write what is called a dissenting opinion. They have the opportunity to explain why they think the majority Supreme Court decision is wrong.

In addition to the federal court system, each state has its own system of courts. These systems vary from state to state. However, they are usually made up of two or three levels of lower courts and then the state's highest court, usually called the state supreme court. Those who lose their cases in the state supreme court may appeal those decisions to the federal court system, usually to the Supreme Court.

Not all cases that are appealed to the Supreme Court are heard by it. In fact, very few of them are. For the Supreme Court to decide to hear a case, four of the nine justices must vote to hear it. If fewer than four justices vote to hear the case, then the judgment of the lower court remains in effect.

The Eighth Amendment

The Eighth Amendment protects the rights of persons suspected or convicted of committing crimes. A *suspected* person may, or may not, be guilty. He or she is still to be judged. A *convicted* person has already been judged. He or she has been found guilty. Therefore, the Eighth Amendment covers quite different types of cases. And the manner of deciding these cases must be quite different. But no matter who the defendant (the accused person) is, the Eighth Amendment says that the rules must be followed when a judge makes a decision. Its primary concern is to see that justice is done when defendants are released or punished.

PHILIP A. KLINKNER

Why the Eighth Amendment?

"That excessive Baile ought not to be required nor excessive Fines imposed nor cruele and unusuale Punishments inflicted."

ENGLISH BILL OF RIGHTS, 1689

The Eighth Amendment is one article of the Bill of Rights. It therefore takes its place among the first ten amendments to the Constitution, which were added to protect the personal rights of American citizens against the government. The Eighth Amendment to the Constitution states the following:

Excessive bail shall not be required, nor excessive fines imposed, nor cruel and unusual punishments inflicted.

The Meaning of the Eighth Amendment

Why is the Eighth Amendment in the Bill of Rights?

The answer is that the Eighth Amendment makes a necessary conclusion to the series of four amendments in the Bill of Rights that concern the citizen's relationship with the judicial system.

George Mason (1725–92) was the American planter and Revolutionary statesman who prepared Virginia's Declaration of Rights in 1776. His criticism of the Constitution was largely responsible for the adoption of the Bill of Rights in 1791. The Eighth Amendment closely follows the wording of clause Number Nine of Virginia's Declaration of Rights.

The Fifth Amendment mentions due process of law as the right of any defendant (accused person) in court. The best-known part of that amendment is a guarantee that a person does not have to testify to anything self-incriminating. Accused people cannot be forced to give evidence against themselves.

The Sixth Amendment concerns criminal prosecutions. Among other things, it calls for quick and public trials. A defendant must be allowed a defense lawyer. There must be an impartial jury. (An impartial jury is one that at the beginning of a trial does not favor one party over another. It is unprejudiced and fair and has not decided the case before it hears the evidence.)

The Seventh Amendment concerns trial by jury in civil cases, those in which the defendant has not committed a crime. (Civil cases are those in which private individuals or businesses sue each other over property or money or are involved in legal disputes about private rights.)

These three amendments deal with the manner in which cases much be handled in court. But what will make sure that a defendant will show up for a trial? And what happens if the defendant is found guilty? Cases often end in convictions, and most convictions call for punishment. These are times when the Eighth Amendment is important.

Part of the Eighth Amendment is about bail. Bail concerns those not yet judged—the defendants who are awaiting trial. Defendants can usually remain free until the trial if they put up bail—a sum of money that they must lose if they do not appear in court.

Part of the Eighth Amendment is about punishment. It concerns the rights of a defendant who has been found guilty.

Fines follow convictions. They are a kind of punishment. They may be imposed as a substitute for jail sentences in the case of the convicted. Or else they may be an addition to other punishments imposed by the court. Legal disputes about fines involve questions such as these: Just how much money makes a fine a fair fine? And how much makes it excessive, that is, too much?

Cruel and unusual punishments are overly harsh penalties. The worst were once common but are now mainly abandoned as inhumane.

Punishment is a necessary part in any legal system. Part of the purpose of the Eighth Amendment is to protect individuals from those government punishments that may be too harsh for the crimes committed. Disputes about the Eighth Amendment have often been ruled on by the lower courts and by the Supreme Court. People have long argued about what is a just punishment. That question has been debated many times and still is a topic of great public interest in the news media. The controversies often have centered on the last phrase in the amendment. That phrase mentions "cruel and unusual punishments."

The Historical Background

The ideas and concepts in the Eighth Amendment have a long history in practical politics. James Madison did not invent the words or even the general ideas of the Eighth Amendment. He studied the past and read documents written long before the United States came into existence.

Magna Carta was the document in which Madison found some of the earliest seeds of the Eighth Amendment. Specifically, he found a condemnation of excessive fines.

Magna Carta (Great Charter) was written during the Middle Ages, a period of history in Britain and Europe from about 450 to 1350. The Middle Ages was a time in which kings ruled in palaces, knights competed in tournaments, archers besieged castles, towns held charters identifying their liberties, and guilds made rules governing their manufactures and trade.

Nobles used Magna Carta to limit the monarch's power. They forced King John I of England to sign it. In doing so, he had to accept limits on his royal power. Magna Carta influenced its own time and provided ideas that would influence later times.

Magna Carta, in spite of its fame, did not set up a democratic system. The English barons who imposed it on King John at Runnymede in 1215 acted in their own interests. They wanted to stop the king from violating their rights in the feudal system. Under the feudal system, the king ruled his barons, and they ruled their knights and tenants on the land. The barons were determined to safeguard their power and their money against officials who ruled in the name of the king. They were aristocrats, not democrats.

And yet, Magna Carta is rightly considered one of the pillars of democracy because in later centuries it came to apply to all the people of England. For example, when the barons mentioned the "law of the land," they meant the medieval law that protected their own rights. However, as the lower classes gained more political power in English society, the "law of the land" was extended to guarantee their rights, too. The old medieval language of Magna Carta was applied to new, modern conditions and helped make Great Britain more democratic.

There is a similarity to the way ideas found in the American Declaration of Independence have been applied to more people over the years. Thomas Jefferson's 1776 statement that "all men are created equal" contradicted political reality in the British colonies and the early United States of his time. Jefferson's words also contradicted his actions, for he was a slave owner. But the statement was flexible enough to cover all men after the Civil War. And 144 years after the Declaration, women finally gained voting rights previously restricted to men. Guided by the Declaration of Independence, the American people developed their democratic system of government.

How is the Eighth Amendment involved in this historical process? Well, one complaint by the English barons against King John was that he forced them to pay very heavy fines. In writing the Eighth Amendment, James Madison agreed that the barons of almost 575 years earlier were correct. But he applied their principle to all citizens of the nation, not just to an upper class. In his view, excessive fines should not be imposed on anyone.

The misuse of fines became an issue during the reign of Charles II of England. In 1682 an official of the city of London insulted the king's brother. A royal court fined the official one hundred thousand pounds—a tremendous fine. Obviously, only a very wealthy man could pay such a fine without being financially ruined. No wonder all exorbitant fines came under attack.

Protection against too-heavy bail is also mentioned in the Eighth Amendment. Madison found information on this point in his study of English history. The question of bail became a heated one in England in the seventeenth century. At that time, the king's officials could keep defendants in jail by denying bail.

During the late 1600s, there was also growing criticism of cruel and unusual punishments imposed by royal judges. The Bloody Assizes of James II's reign horrified many people.

A seventeenth-century execution in the Tower of London. When William and Mary later accepted the throne, they also accepted the English Bill of Rights in 1689. It contained a clause designed to protect against "cruele and unusuale Punishments," but public executions like this one were not considered by most to fall into this category.

The Bloody Assizes were the legal proceedings against men and women who participated in a failed rebellion in 1685. Many people were hanged at public executions. Many were shipped off to the West Indies and forced to work on plantations, from which only death rescued most of them. The use of branding and mutilation was common.

The Bloody Assizes created powerful enemies for the unpopular James II. When he was forced from his throne in 1688, he was accused of a series of crimes against his subjects, everything from royal tyranny to the corruption of justice. The new monarchs, William and Mary, accepted the English Bill of Rights, issued by Parliament in 1689. Among the rights listed were these essential demands: "That excessive Baile ought not to be required nor excessive Fines imposed nor cruele and unusuale Punishments inflicted."

The Virginia Declaration of Rights

The ideas and phrases of the English Bill of Rights crossed the ocean. George Mason had them in mind when he wrote the Virginia Declaration of Rights. That document was adopted shortly before the Declaration of Independence was signed. Dated June 12, 1776, the Virginia Declaration of Rights was a product of the American Revolution. Only the year before, in 1775, the battles of Lexington and Concord had been fought. The Second Continental Congress met and named George Washington to be commander-in-chief of the Continental army. Attempts to reach an agreement with King George III of England failed. The war went on, and the drive toward American independence grew stronger.

The Continental Congress urged the former colonies to change themselves into states with their own state governments. Virginia responded by calling a convention in Williamsburg. Patrick Henry and James Madison were the most famous of the men who attended the convention. But George Mason was the man most responsible for the Virginia Declaration of Rights.

The document had sixteen clauses that laid the foundation for democratic government in the state of Virginia. Number Nine reads: "That excessive bail ought not to be required, nor excessive fines imposed, nor cruel and unusual punishments inflicted."

George Mason had followed the English Bill of Rights word for word. James Madison was present at the convention when the Virginia Declaration of Rights was being debated. He knew the reasons for all the clauses. He was ready to use Mason's Number Nine when the time came for him to write the Eighth Amendment to the Constitution. Most of the other new states included a similar clause in their state constitutions, declarations of rights, or bills of rights.

The Northwest Ordinance of 1787

Before the Bill of Rights was written, another important American document influenced Madison—the Northwest Ordinance of 1787. Between 1781 and the approval of the U.S. Constitution in 1788, the United States was governed by the Continental Congress under a document called the Articles of Confederation. One of the greatest achievements of those years was the passage of the Northwest Ordinance of 1787.

The American Revolution had ended in a peace treaty with Great Britain in 1783. A number of states held claims to the land lying north and west of the Ohio River. Virginia gave up its claim in 1784, and the other states soon gave up their claims. The national government had the problem of deciding what to do about this enormous territory. The debates in Congress led to the Northwest Ordinance of 1787. This law has had a great effect on American history.

The Northwest Ordinance laid down conditions for forming new states in the territory. When any part of the territory had at least 60,000 free men, that part of the territory could apply to Congress for permission to become a state. As a state, the area could have its own government with executive, legislature, and judicial branches.

The first house built in Cincinnati, Ohio, part of the Northwest Territory. The Northwest Ordinance of 1787 contained a bill of rights with a section similar to the Eighth Amendment, which was ratified four years later.

Basic democratic freedoms were guaranteed. That was because the Northwest Ordinance had a bill of rights. (The Northwest Ordinance's rules outlining how regions could become states could be applied far beyond the area for which it was written. New states could be added in the West. In fact, this was done until the United States reached and even crossed part of the Pacific Ocean. In 1959 Alaska and Hawaii entered the Union under the terms provided by the Northwest Ordinance.)

Madison took part in the debates in Congress that resulted in the passage of the Northwest Ordinance. He agreed that the document should include the Second Article, which read: "All persons shall be bailable unless for capital offences, where the proof shall be evident or the presumption [strong belief to be true] great. All fines shall be moderate; and no cruel or unusual punishments shall be inflicted." Capital crimes are serious crimes for which the death penalty may be imposed.

Madison had witnessed the drafting of two great democratic documents—the Virginia Declaration of Rights of 1776 and the Northwest Ordinance of 1787. He had thought long and hard about the problems of bail, fines, and cruel and unusual punishments. His most important achievements regarding these problems still awaited him. They came in 1789 when he wrote the Bill of Rights, including the Eighth Amendment, and in 1791, when the Bill of Rights was approved by the states.

CHAPTER

Jail or Bail

"Nothing in the text of the Bail Clause limits permissible government considerations [whether to allow a defendant to go free on bail before a trial] solely to questions of flight. . . . [T]he Eighth Amendment does not require release on bail."

CHIEF JUSTICE WILLIAM H. REHNQUIST, in *United States* v. *Salerno* (1987)

"**E**xcessive bail shall not be required. . . ."

With these words, the Eighth Amendment sets a rule for the period between a defendant's first appearance in court and the final appearance to hear the verdict from the jury. The rule also applies between a conviction and sentencing and while the defendant files an appeal against the judgment of the court.

The Meaning of Bail

The reason for bail is that cases cannot be decided on the spot. A person who is arrested goes through many stages in the judicial process before acquittal or conviction and sentencing. Bail covers this entire period.

Consider a typical case that will show the steps in the legal proceedings against an accused person. Suppose a man or woman is

Bail bond agents provide an important service for defendants who cannot come up with the money for bail. A bail bond is a three-party contract that involves the state, the accused, and the bail bond agent. The agent guarantees the state that the accused will appear in court at the specified time. If the accused fails to show up in court, the bond agent ends up paying to the court the money specified in the order fixing bail.

suspected of a crime and then arrested by the police and taken to the police station. The next day he or she appears before a judge for a preliminary hearing. A decision is made whether the arrested person should be held for further investigation. If so, a grand jury may meet to evaluate the evidence against him or her. If the grand jury decides that there is enough evidence for a trial, it agrees to an indictment presented by the prosecutor. An indictment is a grand jury's written accusation that the person named has committed a crime.

Where lesser crimes are concerned, an information is used instead of a grand jury indictment. An information is a written accusation presented to the court not by a grand jury but by a public official such as a public prosecutor. It charges the accused with a crime.

If a trial is called for, the accused is ordered to return to court for an arraignment. An arraignment is the process in which the accused person is brought before a court to plead to the criminal charge against him or her. The accused person is asked to plead guilty or not guilty.

After an indictment or information and the arraignment leading to a trial, bail is considered. When a judge orders bail, the accused hands over a sum of money to guarantee his or her appearance at the trial. The accused person returns for the trial and is tried. A verdict of guilty or not guilty is given. The bail money is then handed back to him or her.

Bail is not punishment. If a defendant is considered trustworthy, he or she may be released simply on a promise to be in court on a specified date. This freedom until the hearing is called "release on his or her own recognizance." In other words, the defendant is responsible for himself or herself. A defendant may also be allowed this temporary release on the pledge of a second person, usually a relative or friend. This second person guarantees the appearance of the defendant in court. The second person also agrees to take the consequences if the defendant fails to show up.

Bail is required when there is some doubt about whether a defendant will keep a promise to come back to court for the hearing. But the judge must believe that the defendant would rather return to court and face the verdict than lose the bail money. Sometimes that belief is not justified. Defendants may use their freedom to escape, or to "skip bail." When that happens, they obviously have little chance of being granted bail again. If captured, they will go to jail.

The bail money may be put up by the defendant or by somebody else who is willing to trust him or her. If the sum is large, a bail bond agent generally produces the money. A bail bond agent is paid a fee for finding the money to gain temporary release for defendants. The bail bond agent usually has to make a decision about whether to trust the accused man or woman. The big question is, Can this person, the defendant, be trusted when somebody else's money is at stake?

Before making a decision, the bail bond agent will find out everything he or she can about the defendant's character, background, and circumstances. If the defendant seems reliable, is said to be a good citizen, and is in trouble with the law for the first time, the defendant will probably receive the bail money. If the defendant has a bad record—multiple crimes, for instance—a bail bond agent may well refuse to put up the required bail. Too much money is at stake to take a chance.

The Importance of Bail

The Supreme Court ruled in *Schilb* v. *Kuebel* (1971) that "[b]ail, of course, is basic to our system of law." Why is this? There are a number of reasons. The following four are almost always taken into account.

First, there is the possibility that the defendant will be found not guilty after returning for the trial. The purpose of bail in this case is to prevent an innocent person from going to jail while awaiting trial.

Second, there may be hardships for the family should bail be denied. The defendant may be needed at home during the period before his or her court appearance.

Third, social problems might be caused by a denial of bail. Thus, the defendant might meet suspicion or even hostility from colleagues in the workplace who know about his or her pretrial time behind bars.

Fourth, the defendant may need free time to look for necessary documents, consult a lawyer, and do whatever else is necessary to prepare the strongest possible defense.

When is bail fair? When is it set at the right amount? These are difficult questions because judges follow their own ideas on the subject. Disagreement is inevitable. One judge will set high bail when another judge would be more lenient.

Some critics of the system would like to see a uniform code for defendants who qualify for bail. The same charge would then carry the same bail for all defendants. The trouble is that nobody has been able to draw up such a complete code.

It seems impossible to put a single price tag on all cases where one kind of charge is involved. The charge of auto theft is a good example. Too many details are unique in each case of this crime. Who claims to have seen the defendant? Are the so-called witnesses friends or enemies of the defendant? And so on. The facts cannot be identical in any two cases, let alone in all of them. As a result, there appears to be no fair alternative to letting judges decide as they see fit within certain guidelines.

The Eighth Amendment prohibits excessive bail, but how are we to understand the word *excessive*? Most people agree that the sum should be large enough to prevent the defendant from walking out of the courtroom and not returning. Everyone agrees it should *not* be so large that the defendant cannot raise it. That would amount to bail denied.

One danger is that the poor may be unable to get bail. Since they cannot raise the money themselves, they are often dependent on bail bond agents. And bail bond agents may be unwilling to help if they are not reasonably sure of receiving their fees.

A judge will take this problem into consideration. Officers of the court and social workers will be asked to tell what they know about the defendant's character. If the reports are favorable, the chances are that the judge will not set any bail for minor crimes. The judge will stretch the point and release the defendant "upon his own recognizance." If the reports are very unfavorable, bail will be set, even though the defendant cannot raise it. The defendant will be held in jail.

Bail and Crime

Serious crimes call for high bail. If a judge sets bail at one hundred thousand dollars for someone accused of stealing millions of dollars from a bank, this would scarcely be considered too high. On the other hand, it would certainly be excessive for someone who passed a single bad check for eighty dollars at a department store.

Bail is usually not allowed in the most serious crimes of all: brutal murder and rape cases. The alleged criminals, if guilty, will probably not stick around to hear themselves sentenced to long prison terms or, perhaps, to death. Denial of bail is often based on the fear that, while free, they might commit the same crime again.

However, even murder does not always cause bail to be denied. Bail is often available in cases of crimes of passion, when one person kills another in a fit of anger. This kind of murder is not committed in cold blood. The murderer does not plan the crime but strikes in a moment of uncontrollable rage. This type of murder sometimes happens in family quarrels, and the murderer is often conscience-stricken. He or she probably will never do anything like that again and is not a danger to society. Therefore bail is set, and he or she goes free until the trial.

The Eighth Amendment states that bail is not to be excessive, but it does not give any guidance about what this means. The amendment does not define the word *excessive*. The problem was left to judges sitting on the bench and struggling to make common-sense decisions on the cases before them. Therefore, many judges made many rulings and contradicted one another about the meaning of excessive bail.

Today, judges have much assistance that was not available when the Eighth Amendment was written. In *Stack* v. *Boyle* (1951), the Supreme Court offered some guidelines for judges to follow. The justices noted that the purpose of bail is to make sure that accused persons will appear in court. The justices then said that bail money demanded by judges would be excessive if "set at a figure higher than an amount reasonably calculated." In other words, bail should be just high enough to "reasonably" make sure of the defendant's return to court, but no higher.

Congress has passed measures to clarify the use of bail. The Bail Reform Act of 1966 stated that bail could be denied to defendants accused of crimes punishable by death. In lesser crimes, judges could deny bail if they had good reason to believe that a defendant might flee. If no such fear existed, then bail could not be denied.

One of the purposes of the 1966 law was to make sure that poor defendants would be treated fairly. Over the years, the law ran into repeated complaints. Some thought that too many people accused of crimes were allowed bail and therefore were not being held in prison before their trials. Critics of the law claimed that it did not give judges enough power to deny bail to defendants who probably intended to flee or who were dangerous to the community. People wanted a law that protected the community from the criminal activities of defendants who might be released on bail.

In response to such criticism, Congress passed the Bail Reform Act of 1984. This law repealed the 1966 law's rules, which had given people the right to reasonable bail in almost all noncapital cases.

In the Bail Reform Act of 1984, Congress withdrew the right to bail for all crimes not punishable by death. This act gave judges freedom to deny bail to defendants who might become a danger to society. In addition, the congressional guidelines allowed judges to set a number of conditions for those to be set free on bail. The defendants might be compelled to obey a curfew limiting the hours they could leave their houses. They could be ordered not to carry guns, knives, or other dangerous weapons. They could be ordered to avoid becoming drunk. They could be ordered to stay away from persons who might be witnesses against them. The purpose of this order was to prevent defendants from threatening witnesses. These guidelines gave more freedom to judges.

Pretrial Detention and the Bail Reform Act of 1984

The Bail Reform Act of 1984 also allows the judge to order detention of the defendant before trial. The accused, under certain circumstances, can therefore be held in prison without bail. The 1984 law outlines the rules about pretrial detention. A hearing must be held before pretrial detention is imposed. Pretrial detention is possible if the person is accused of a crime of violence or of a serious crime that could lead to life imprisonment or the death penalty. Pretrial detention is possible if the defendant is accused of a drug crime punishable by at least ten years in prison. Pretrial detention is also possible if the defendant is accused of any serious crime after the person has already been convicted two or more times for certain kinds of serious crimes. The result has been that the law allows judges to deny bail more frequently.

The Bail Reform Act of 1984 was soon challenged in court. In 1986 Anthony Salerno and Vincent Cafaro were arrested. They were thought to be members of organized crime. The two were charged with various criminal activities including mail fraud, extortion, gambling, and conspiracy to commit murder. The government demanded that they be held in pretrial detention. The basis for this demand was the Bail Reform Act of 1984. The law directs that the setting of bail take into account the protection of community safety.

The U.S. district court held a hearing and heard court-ordered wiretap evidence that the two men had planned to use violence in their illegal activities. The U.S. district court decided that pretrial detention would be all right in this case.

The defendants appealed their case to the U.S. court of appeals. They claimed that to put them in prison before a trial on the grounds that they *might* commit *future* crimes was unconstitutional. The U.S. court of appeals agreed with them.

The government didn't like that decision and so appealed the case to the Supreme Court. In *United States* v. *Salerno* (1987), the Court ruled against Salerno and Cafaro, reversing the judgment of the U.S. court of appeals. Chief Justice William H. Rehnquist delivered the majority opinion:

> Respondents [Salerno and Cafaro] first argue that the act violates . . . due process because the pretrial detention it authorizes constitutes impermissible punishment before trial. . . . The Government, however, has never argued that pretrial detention could be upheld if it were "punishment.". . .
>
> Respondents also contend that the Bail Reform Act violates the Excessive Bail Clause of the Eighth Amendment. . . .
>
> The Eighth Amendment addresses pretrial release by providing merely that "Excessive bail shall not be required." This Clause, of course, says nothing about whether bail shall be available at all. Respondents nevertheless contend [argue] that this Clause grants them a right to bail calculated solely on considerations of flight. . . . In respondents' view, since the Bail Reform Act allows a court essentially to set bail at an infinite amount for reasons not related to flight, it violates the Excessive Bail Clause.
>
> Nothing in the text of the Bail Clause limits permissible government considerations solely to questions of flight.

This Supreme Court ruling meant that some accused people could be denied bail and held in jail to prevent them from becoming a danger to other people. How long can a person not yet tried and not yet found guilty be held in pretrial detention? The Speedy Trial Act of 1982 set a limit. In most cases, a defendant can be held in pretrial detention for only ninety days.

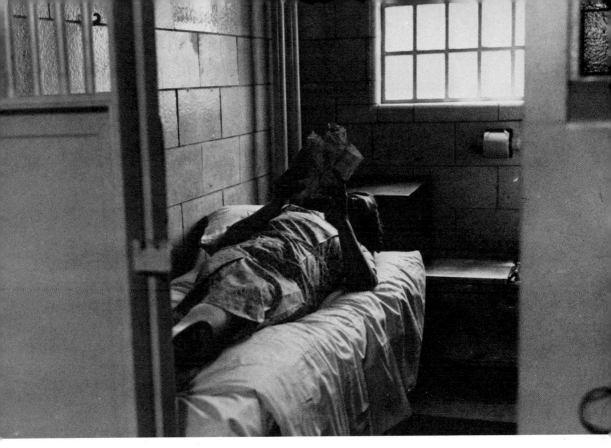

The Eighth Amendment protects citizens against excessive bail. However, there is no constitutional right to bail as an alternative to prison while awaiting trial.

Justices Thurgood Marshall, William J. Brennan, Jr., and John P. Stevens disagreed with the Court's majority opinion in *United States* v. *Salerno* (1987). In his dissenting opinion, Justice Marshall asked what would happen if someone was held in pretrial detention and was then found not guilty:

But our fundamental principles of justice declare that the defendant is as innocent on the day before his trial as he is on the morning after his acquittal. Under this statute [the Bail Reform Act of 1984] an untried indictment somehow acts to permit detention, based on other charges, which after an acquittal would be unconstitutional. The conclusion is inescapable that the indictment has been turned into evidence, if not that the defendant is guilty of the crime charged, then that left to his own devices he will soon be guilty of something else.

Honoring the presumption of innocence [the belief that a person is innocent of any crime until proven guilty] is often difficult; sometimes we must pay substantial social costs as a result of our commitment to the values we espouse [support].

Some states acted quickly on the *United States* v. *Salerno* ruling. In 1988 New Mexico allowed denial of bail to individuals considered dangerous in the period between conviction and appeal. Oklahoma gave judges the right to deny bail where dangerous repeat offenders were concerned, even in crimes less serious than murder and rape.

In 1990 a Georgia judge showed how bail can be denied and granted in the same case. The characters of two codefendants made the difference. They were a husband and wife suspected by the Georgia police of bombings that killed two people. Both co-defendants were accused of perjury (lying under oath) and obstruction of justice.

A judge in Macon, Georgia, denied bail to the husband. The judge said the defendant was "a danger to the community and if not controlled could be expected to attempt to retaliate against [get even with] or tamper with witnesses against him." This defendant was held without bail.

His wife, on the contrary, was set free on bail because the judge felt she was not "a serious threat to others." The Georgia authorities believed that the wife was unlikely to become violent as long as she was separated from her husband.

High Bail

Bail can also be set so high that it amounts to denial of bail. In 1990 a judge in Los Angeles set bail at 2 million dollars for the son of actor Marlon Brando. The son was charged with murder. The judge said he did this to make sure the defendant would not skip bail.

Why not simply deny bail in such cases? Often the judge believes that if a very large sum is raised, the person who stands to lose it will keep an eye on the defendant. There will be little or no chance of the defendant escaping. If the defendant is not likely to become violent outside the courtroom, then his or her high-priced temporary freedom may be justified.

Besides the Supreme Court and Congress, private groups have come forward to help with the problem of bail. The Manhattan Bail Project of 1961 focused on pretrial evidence. A group of reformers in New York argued that the differences between defendants were not sufficiently understood. These reformers began gathering information about individuals from relatives, friends, doctors, and other knowledgeable people. They drew up statistics, wrote scientific studies, and made what they learned available to the courts. As a result, judges could understand defendants better. Judges could safely set lower bail for many defendants and take the word of other defendants that they would return for trial without bail.

Defendants who feel they are being treated unfairly can ask support from such groups as the National Council of Social Work, the Children's Aid Society, and the National Organization for Women (NOW). These groups often go into court to speak for defendants when constitutional issues are being debated. With the information these groups provide, judges are better able to consider social factors. These include home conditions, psychological problems, and medical history. Such new factors available to courts are sometimes hard to judge. However, they do throw light on the reasons why defendants are standing before judges at all. If juveniles are in trouble, social workers from the Children's Aid Society may come into court to testify about problems at home or in the streets. If women are in trouble because of abuse at home, NOW may be able to help with information about their marriage problems. If men become alcoholics or criminals, psychologists may look into their mental condition and point to depression or tension as the root cause. These experts are a big help to judges since they have to pass sentences on other human beings.

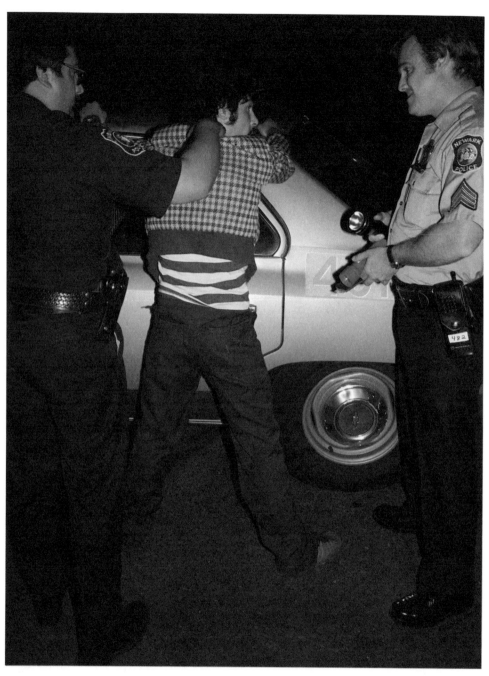

A suspect apprehended. The Eighth Amendment protects the accused against being required to pay excessive bail in cases involving the federal government. It does not protect citizens against excessive bail imposed on them by state or local authorities.

Bail has many problems, and many questions must be asked before it is decided in a particular case. Suppose a woman has committed murder. With regard to bail, the first question is the nature of the crime. Was it a crime of passion or carefully planned and deliberate? Is there any danger the defendant will flee if allowed out on bail? Will she obey the court order to return for trial? Is there a strong possibility that she will be a threat to society? Will other prisoners be a threat to her if bail is denied and she is put into prison? Will her reputation suffer if a stay in jail becomes public knowledge? It takes professional knowledge to answer these questions properly. The information provided by experts is needed by judges who decide on bail.

Great problems remain. Still, there can be no doubt that excessive bail is now demanded by judges less often. The ideal of the Eighth Amendment is closer to reality than it used to be.

CHAPTER 3

Proper Fines

"[P]enalties can be imposed for negligence, substantial understatement of tax, and fraud. Criminal penalties may be imposed for willful failure to file, tax evasion, or making a false statement."

DEPARTMENT OF THE TREASURY, INTERNAL REVENUE SERVICE,
1040 Forms and Instructions

"**N**or excessive fines imposed . . ."

With these words, the Eighth Amendment sets a rule for punishment after conviction. In using the word *excessive,* the Eighth Amendment repeats what is said about bail. With regard to a fine, a judge is warned against setting a penalty that does not match the defendant's action. The punishment should fit the crime.

The Meaning of Fines

When Magna Carta was signed in 1215, the English barons forbade King John to levy fines that would make it impossible for accused persons to maintain their standard of living. This remained an ideal. If possible, a fine should hurt without financially ruining the accused.

The great historical documents that followed Magna Carta supported the right of individuals not to be bankrupted by fines. True, the documents did not say so. But that was how the phrase

---

A fine is a money payment that a person convicted of an offense is required to pay. The Supreme Court has never made a major ruling defining what fines are excessive and what are not. Local laws often set forth the lower and upper limits of fines.

"excessive fines" came to be understood. Each document reflected the social conditions of its own time. The Virginia Declaration of Rights in 1776 meant that those who were fined should be able to carry on their lives as planters, farmers, and craftspeople of Virginia. In their state constitution and state declarations or bills of rights, other states from New Hampshire to North Carolina forbade fines that would financially disrupt the lives of workers.

The Bill of Rights in 1791 applied this concept to protection against actions by the government of the United States. The population of the whole country was much more varied than that of any single state. The guarantee against excessive fines meant that all the landowners, shopkeepers, farmers, and workers could depend on the Eighth Amendment for protection against federal fines that might bankrupt them. That guarantee is still available to the American people.

A fine is a penalty for wrongdoing. The convicted person stands condemned of breaking the law or doing some damage that is not a crime. The fine is the judge's way of making people pay for their acts. The word "pay" is literal. The accused hands over a sum of money, when the amount of the fine has been decided, and goes free. He or she is not subject to another fine for the same crime. But what if a person cannot pay the fine? This is a danger to the poor, who may suffer in two ways. Any sum of money may be too much for a poor individual to pay. Or the individual, facing a decision between a fine or going to jail, may choose to go to jail. The states provide remedies for this. The poor may simply not be fined. They may work off the penalty in community service or in some other activity that makes up for the fine.

Even those who are not poor can find themselves in a difficult situation. An individual who can pay a moderate fine without difficulty, will be unable to pay if the fine is beyond his or her means. What is excessive for one man or woman is not excessive for another.

Unlike bail, fines do not require a reappearance in court. The accused is sentenced on the spot, pays the fine, and leaves. The great majority of fines concern minor violations of the law. Those who pay are lesser criminals and therefore are often not subject to any other punishment.

Driving over the speed limit, hunting without a license, driving without a safety belt—these are typical of violations that may call for small fines only.

Typical Fines

Penalties for these violations of the law can frequently be set according to simple steps upward, from ten dollars to a hundred dollars or so. Suppose a judge confronts five defendants accused of misusing their cars. The five fines might look like this:

- $10 for overparking
- $25 for driving without a seat belt
- $50 for speeding
- $75 for running a stop light
- $100 for driving in the wrong lane

In such cases, there is something approaching an automatic list of fines judges have in their heads. They can impose the same fines over and over again. A number of judges might have different price lists, but nearly all would rate the infractions in the above order.

There is almost no chance of these small fines being called excessive. Most people would probably agree that they are proper fines for the individuals who must pay them.

Local ordinances and laws often set forth the lower and upper limits of fines. On the national level, the Internal Revenue Service lists penalties.

Violations more serious than overparking or walking a dog without a leash are more difficult to list. How much of a fine should a hit-and-run driver be forced to pay? How much for drunk driving? How much for selling illegal drugs? How much for car theft?

There is no agreement about such cases. Charges that fines are excessive are often made by lawyers representing defendants in court. On the other hand, some fines may seem too mild to prosecuting attorneys, lawyers who present the government's case against defendants.

The problem becomes more difficult when a second penalty is added. Both sides might accept a low fine if a judge sets a jail term as well as a fine. The meaning of "low fine" would then have to be decided. How many dollars against how many days in jail? Judges have differed markedly in answering that question.

What is regarded as excessive can differ from community to community. It certainly varies from country to country as shown in a recent study of punishments for drunken driving. Some nations imposed more than a small fine:

- *Australia:* Names sent to newspapers and published under the title "He's Drunk and in Jail."
- *Bulgaria:* Second conviction can mean execution.
- *Costa Rica:* License plates taken by police.
- *El Salvador:* First offense could lead to execution by firing squad.
- *England:* One-year suspension of license, about $250 in fines, and one year in jail.
- *Finland and Sweden:* Automatic sentence of one year in jail at hard labor.
- *France:* Three years' loss of license, one year in jail, and about $1,000 in fines.
- *Malaysia:* Driver is jailed and spouse can be jailed also.
- *Norway:* Three weeks in jail at hard labor and one year's loss of license. For second offense within five years, license is revoked for life.
- *South Africa:* Ten-year prison sentence and/or a $10,000 fine.
- *USSR:* License revoked for life.

Crime by business executives during the 1980s produced a bizarre situation with regard to fines. Multimillion dollar fines were often condemned as too mild.

Congress Acts

In 1986 the Securities and Exchange Commission, a government agency, fined Ivan Boesky one hundred million dollars. Boesky was a Wall Street investor found guilty of a serious crime called the misuse of insider information. The law says that those in a position to learn about confidential corporate deals may not use that knowledge for their own profit. The reason is that such individuals have an advantage over the public. Those on the outside, not having this insider information, cannot profit.

Boesky used insider information about planned corporate mergers to make deals for himself. He passed insider information on to some acquaintances who were able to act on it. They all raked in enormous profits. When Boesky was exposed, he confessed. Other Wall Street employees were caught in the same net. Some of them also received multimillion dollar fines.

In 1987 a judge, saying it was impossible to "forgive and forget," added a prison sentence to Boesky's fine. This was a common fate for other defendants in the insider trading scandal on Wall Street.

Yet, the multimillion dollar fines were often condemned as too low. Some members of the public and the news media feel that a fine of many millions is too low if the guilty party has a fortune squirreled away. The suspicion arose that some defendants had enough money in secret Swiss bank accounts to remain wealthy after getting out of jail.

Stung by all this, Congress passed the Insider Trading and Securities Fraud Act of 1988. Crimes involving users of insider information often began with workers on Wall Street. Congress

A truck at a weigh station. Operators of trucks that weigh more than the amount allowed on certain highways can be fined. The safeguard against excessive fines is one of the few rights in the Bill of Rights that still applies only to fines imposed by the federal government. There is no federal constitutional protection against excessive fines that might be imposed by state or local governments.

therefore increased mandatory fines (those that judges must impose) on companies that "knowingly or recklessly" failed to supervise their workers.

Of course there were people who knew what was going on but were not directly involved. They were encouraged to come forward and testify against the criminals. These informers were promised 10 percent of the fines.

The Supreme Court has never made a major ruling on fines—on what fines are excessive and what are not.

Cruel and Unusual Punishments

"The principle that a punishment should be proportionate to the crime is deeply rooted and frequently repeated in common-law jurisprudence."

JUSTICE LEWIS F. POWELL, JR., in *Solem* v. *Helm* (1983)

"Nor cruel and unusual punishments inflicted."

With these words, the Eighth Amendment takes up the question of what to do with people convicted of crimes too serious to allow for their release after a mere fine. They are criminals who, in the view of the authorities, must suffer personally for what they have done.

This question is as old as humanity. Crimes have always been committed, and people have always tried to punish the criminals. Archaeologists have found the remains of executed criminals preserved in the earth for thousands of years. Ancient texts such as the Bible describe crimes and punishments. Crimes and punishments have been part of the human experience.

The Meaning of Cruel and Unusual Punishments

To what kind of punishments should criminals be subjected? Over the centuries, human beings have thought up a long list, some so

The pillory was a device commonly used in colonial New England to publicly punish offenders. It consisted of a wooden frame with holes in which the head and hands could be locked. It was used to expose the wrong-doers to public scorn and ridicule.

horrible we can scarcely believe anyone ever used them. Some are mentioned in the Code of Hammurabi, who ruled in Babylon nearly 3,800 years ago. This code is notable for punishments based on the principle of "an eye for an eye," which is also found in many other ancient codes. For example, in the book of Exodus (21.23-25) it is stated: "And if any mischief follow, then thou shalt give life for life, eye for eye, tooth for tooth, burning for burning, wound for wound, stripe for stripe." The meaning is that criminals should pay in kind for what they have done. They should suffer the same injuries that they have inflicted on others. In reality, scholars have shown that even in biblical times payments were often substituted for physical punishments. Yet mutilations, especially in Europe, were justified for centuries on the basis of this biblical text.

Many horrible punishments were developed. The Bible records stoning, crucifixion, and dismemberment. The Romans threw early Christians to the lions. Almost anything that could cause pain seems to have been considered right for punishing some crimes. This was especially the case because the few who ruled often used force and fear when their rule was not based on the consent of the governed.

The fate of Joan of Arc reveals one of the worst sides of medieval law. Joan led the French to victory over the English in the Hundred Years War. She was captured and turned over to a court for judgment. Condemned as a witch and a heretic—a person who opposes basic religious doctrines—she received a death sentence and went to the stake in 1431. She suffered the agony of being engulfed in flames.

The Spanish Inquisition used torture and execution by burning at the stake. The Inquisition was set up to discover and punish religious heretics. Prisoners were often placed on the rack, a wooden frame that held them by the wrists and ankles. The rack could be lengthened by twisting ropes, the result being that the victims were pulled in two directions until they suffered broken bones. The thumbscrew crushed the thumb. The iron boot crushed the foot. And these were only a few of the horrors that went on in Inquisition prisons.

This is an eighteenth-century engraving of a torture chamber used by the Spanish Inquisition in earlier centuries. It illustrates a variety of cruel tortures.

These examples of torture could be multiplied across Europe. Some were still being used until a couple of centuries ago. Of course, torture was widely used around the world. It ranged from strangling with a rope in the Middle East to the death of a thousand cuts in Asia. No area of the globe held a monopoly on horribly painful punishments.

But we should not think this is all in the past. Amnesty International reported in 1990 that many nations are still using torture against captured enemies, rebels, and human rights activists. Severe beatings, burnings, starvation, and imprisonment in complete darkness are only too common in our time. Amnesty International was founded to expose and stop cruel and unusual punishments. Its workers investigate problems in many countries around the world.

This engraving illustrates methods of torture applied in the Tower of London. The rack was an instrument of torture on which a person was stretched.

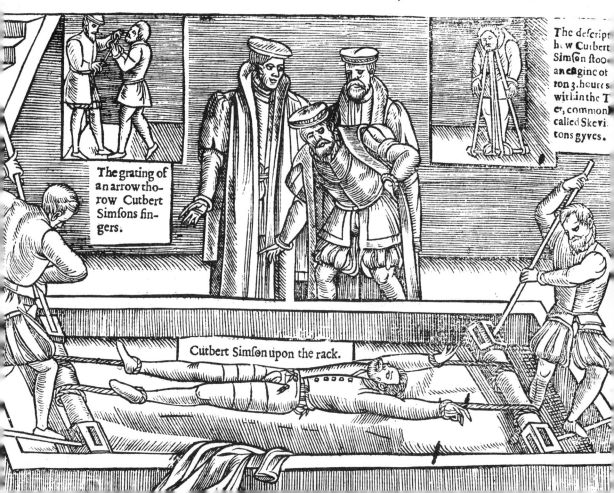

With regard to the United States and its Eighth Amendment, which outlaws cruel and unusual punishments, the Americans started with one advantage. The British colonies possessed more humane punishment systems than Europe did. This was partly due to wise colonial governors. William Penn is the most famous. When Penn founded Pennsylvania, he drew up a plan for his colony that outlawed torture. He allowed the death penalty for murder and treason only.

The Witchcraft Delusion

Massachusetts used the death penalty during the Salem witchcraft delusion of 1692. A group of girls accused many women and a few men of being witches. These women were said to have put a curse on their victims. They were accused of getting their power from the Devil. In the superstitious atmosphere of Salem, most of the accused had little hope of a fair trial. About twenty were found guilty of consorting with the Devil. All were hanged except one unfortunate who was crushed to death under heavy weights. More than a hundred people went to jail.

Eventually the people of Salem came to their senses. They felt sorry for the horrors committed during the witch delusion. Milder punishments similar to those of other colonies were applied to criminals now that the Devil no longer haunted the imaginations of those who enforced justice in Salem. In contrast, in Europe in the 1500s, 1600s, and 1700s, hundreds of thousands of women were put to death for witchcraft.

Even milder punishments could be unpleasant. The pillory was a wooden frame with openings for the head and wrists when the top was raised. When the top was lowered, the convicted criminal could not get free. He or she had to stand in place for the time set by the judge's sentence. The stocks, fastened over the ankles, held the feet in a similar manner.

This German woodcut shows the public burning of three women convicted of witchcraft in 1555. Very few people were put to death for witchcraft in the American colonies; hundreds of thousands were killed as witches in Europe.

Branding and the lash continued to be used in an effort to control violent crime. The death penalty remained in all the colonies for the worst crimes, especially murder.

Even the English Bill of Rights (1689), while it outlawed cruel and unusual punishments, still allowed things we would not tolerate today. A young child convicted of theft might be beaten or imprisoned. A woman who stole a hat or a man who took fish from an aristocrat's pond might be sent to labor on plantations in the West Indies.

The Humanitarian Movement

A new era began in Europe in the eighteenth century. A number of writers, philosophers, and political reformers launched an attack on brutal punishments. Their leader was Cesare Beccaria, an Italian law professor who published *On Crimes and Punishments* in 1764. Beccaria denounced torture, not only because it was cruel, but also because it was so often useless. He pointed out that it caused innocent people to confess to crimes they never committed.

The French writer Voltaire ridiculed the punishments of the time in his comedy *Candide.* Voltaire condemned the authorities in the case of Jean Calas, who was tortured and burned on a charge of murdering his son. Calas was later declared to be not guilty. People were shaken by the horrid treatment of an innocent man, and the use of torture found fewer defenders.

People brought these ideas from the European humanitarian movement across the Atlantic and helped to make American thinking more humane. In 1776 Virginia became the first state to protect its citizens against cruel and unusual punishments. Six other states soon wrote this protection into their Revolutionary constitutions and declarations or bills of rights. And that brings us to the U.S. Constitution, the Bill of Rights, and the Eighth Amendment.

For two centuries, judges, lawyers, and legislators have taken it for granted that the cruel and unusual punishment clause of the Eighth Amendment forbids brutalities. Almost all the cases on which the Supreme Court has ruled have involved mild punishments—that is, mild in comparison with the punishments inflicted in earlier times. In almost all cases, the sentences imposed by lower courts have been allowed to stand.

In 1972 Justice William Brennan noted in a dissenting opinion in *Furman* v. *Georgia*: "Since the Bill of Rights was adopted, this Court has adjudged [declared] only three punishments to be within the prohibition of the clause." He meant that these three were not allowed under the Eighth Amendment. The cases are as follows:

1. *Weems* v. *United States* (1910). A defendant had been sentenced by a lower court to twelve to twenty years at hard and painful labor for being an accessory to the falsification of a public document.

2. *Trop* v. *Dulles* (1958). A defendant had been sentenced by a lower court to lose his citizenship after conviction on a charge of wartime desertion.

3. *Robinson* v. *California* (1962). A defendant had been sentenced by a lower court to prison for narcotics addiction.

The Supreme Court declared all three punishments to be cruel and unusual. It therefore reversed the sentences as violations of the Eighth Amendment. Sentences like these would have gone unchallenged in earlier times. Why, then, were they challenged in the twentieth century? And why did the Supreme Court reject such sentences?

Changing Ideas of Justice

The answer lies in the way ideas of justice change over time. Ideas of right and wrong do not remain as they are as the years pass. What is acceptable at one period becomes unacceptable at another. History has seen this happen with torture, slavery, and the subjection of women. All of these are condemned today, regardless of what anyone said in the past. As Chief Justice Earl Warren said in the majority opinion in *Trop* v. *Dulles* (1958), the Eighth Amendment "must draw its meaning from the evolving [changing] standards of decency that mark the progress of a maturing society."

The fundamental question is plain. What standards of decency apply today?

The Supreme Court had made its reply in *Weems* v. *United States* (1910): "Today the Eighth Amendment prohibits punishments which, although not physically barbarous, involve the unnecessary and wanton [intentional and reckless] infliction of pain, or are grossly disproportionate to the severity of the crime." Disproportionate means the punishment does not fit the crime. The

Supreme Court attacked this problem in three important decisions. These rulings show the justices developing guidelines for appeals under the heading of disproportionate sentences.

Corporal punishment was an expected way of disciplining students in the United States in the nineteenth century. A 1977 Supreme Court ruling stated that common law permits public school officials to give out only such punishment as is reasonably necessary for the proper education and discipline of a child. Any punishment beyond that might result in civil lawsuits or even criminal charges.

In *Rummel* v. *Estelle* (1980), the defendant committed three crimes in Texas during a nine-year period. He was found guilty of fraud in using a credit card, of cashing bad checks, and of obtaining money under false pretenses. He gained less than $300 from his crimes. Texas law allowed a life sentence for a criminal convicted of three separate crimes. That was the sentence handed down by a Texas court in this case.

The defense, in appealing to the Supreme Court, claimed it was cruel and unusual punishment to sentence Rummel to life when the crimes he committed were nonviolent. The Supreme Court rejected this appeal. In its majority opinion, delivered by Chief Justice William H. Rehnquist, the Court held that states have a right to make laws to curb repeat offenders. The justices also said that life sentences can be a justifiable way of doing this, even in the case of nonviolent crimes. The Court's conclusion was that the sentence in *Rummel* v. *Estelle* was not disproportionate.

The same argument applied in *Hutto* v. *Davis* (1981). This defendant was sentenced to forty years for possessing nine ounces of marijuana. The Supreme Court took into account the fact that marijuana is a drug that can be both used by an individual and sold by him. The Court refused to support the appeal and said the sentence was not disproportionate. As in *Rummel* v. *Estelle*, the justices left the decisions in particular cases to the states.

However, the Supreme Court ruled differently in *Solem* v. *Helm* (1983). The defendant had a number of crimes on his record in South Dakota. They were all minor, such as thefts of small amounts of money. Then he was caught passing a bad check. He was sentenced under a South Dakota law regarding recidivists—criminals who do not reform after repeated punishment. They return to a life of crime. More than 62 percent of state prisoners who are released from prison are rearrested after three years. More than 41 percent are reconvicted.

Under South Dakota's recidivist law, the defendant received a life sentence without possibility of parole. This meant he could not hope for a reduction of his sentence for good behavior. The

Supreme Court called the sentence disproportionate and reversed it. Justice Lewis F. Powell, Jr., wrote the majority opinion. He stated that *Solem* v. *Helm* was "fundamentally different from the Texas law [*Rummel* v. *Estelle*] because it completely banned the possibility of parole." This sentence was disproportionate.

At the same time, the justices set forth three tests that should be used in deciding whether a sentence is disproportionate. First, is the sentence too harsh for the crime? Second, has a court given a harsher sentence to one defendant than it has given to others convicted of the same crime? Third, do other courts give similar sentences for similar crimes?

The disproportionate argument does not mean that punishments always get lighter. They may get more severe. The war on drugs has caused harsher penalties by judges and juries because the use of drugs has become a national danger. Those involved in the drug trade are often sentenced to many years in prison, or even life. Lawmakers have passed stricter drug laws. Harsher penalties are thought to fit the crime better than lighter penalties where drugs are concerned.

Punishment and Imprisonment

Imprisonment has been the subject of numerous Supreme Court decisions. This is logical because American prisons hold more than 710,000 prisoners who have a right to appeal against the conditions in which they are held. There are three types of prisons. Minimum security prisons have few guards and generally do not need high walls. They are for prisoners who are trusted to serve their time, learn from their mistakes, take their punishment, and reform. It is believed that they have a good chance to rejoin society as responsible citizens. Some are allowed to leave the prison at certain times because the prison authorities are confident they will return.

Medium security prisons are the most common type. They have many guards, strong walls, and locked gates. They are for prisoners who have committed bad crimes and have to be held behind bars. Some prisoners have committed crimes more than once. But the hope is that all will reform and some will win a reduction of their sentences for good behavior.

Maximum security prisons hold the worst criminals. These criminals have committed violent crimes that may be anything from assault and battery to rape and murder. Many are repeat offenders. Many are imprisoned as dangerous to society. Sentences as long as fifty years or more are common. Life sentences are served in these institutions. All maximum security prisons have strong walls, armed guards, searchlights, and often police dogs.

The most famous maximum security prison was Alcatraz in San Francisco Bay. It held unreformable prisoners including gangsters of the 1920s and 1930s, such as Al Capone. Alcatraz officials said there was no chance for prisoners to escape to freedom because the strong current of the Bay would drown them. Some prisoners got out of the prison, but none is known to have survived the swim across the Bay. Statesville prison in Joliet, Illinois, is considered a model of how maximum security prisons should be built. It has cells in a circle, and the circles rise in stories one above the other. Guards in central towers can see into all the cells and give the alarm if a cell is empty.

Prisoners' Rights

The way prisoners are treated brings appeals to the Supreme Court. In *Johnson* v. *Avery* (1969), the question of prisoners' rights came up. At a prison in Tennessee, the prisoners were forced to stop helping one another in preparing appeals. The Court disallowed this practice. The justices said that the right of appeal is a basic constitutional right, even in prison, and that poorly educated prisoners had a right to assistance with their appeals. In *Bounds* v. *Smith* (1977), the Court went further and said prison authorities must assist prisoners in filing legal papers. Prisoners must be provided with adequate law libraries or help from people trained in the law.

Wolff v. *McDonnell* (1974) dealt with prison discipline. The Court said that prisoners had a right to be informed of changes in prison policy, such as a decision to transfer them from one prison to another. The Court considered the matter of prison cell searches and body searches in *Bell* v. *Wolfish* (1979). Prisoners complained that searches included their cells when they were not there and their bodies after visits by outsiders. Opponents of the searches argued that the constitutional rights of the prisoners were being violated. The Supreme Court rejected the appeal on the ground that prison officials had a right to make the searches because weapons and other forbidden objects might be concealed in the cells or in their bodies.

Prisons replaced most of the brutalities listed earlier in this chapter. When horrible cruelties were abolished, something still had to be done with criminals. Prisons were the main solution. American prisons are models of humane treatment compared with the dungeons of old. Few think we could do without them. But conditions *in* prison and sentences *to* prison have both been criticized as cruel and unusual.

Prison Conditions

Conditions *in* prison concern first of all the number of prisons and the number of prisoners. Both are increasing. As the population of the United States grows, so does the number of Americans who commit crimes. More prisons must be built to hold them. In 1990 there were about 710,000 prisoners in state and federal institutions. There was a need for about 1,600 new bed spaces per week. The problem of putting as many prisoners as possible into existing prisons grew. When a new prison is not yet built, the result can be overcrowding in an old prison.

In 1981 the Supreme Court was asked to decide a case, *Rhodes* v. *Chapman*, in which prisoners were placed two to a cell in cells intended for one. Saying that the Eighth Amendment "does not mandate comfortable prisons,'' the justices denied that there was anything cruel and unusual in this case.

Other prison conditions that have been mentioned in appeals to the Supreme Court concern bad food, dirty cells, violence among prisoners, and poor medical treatment for convicts who are either injured or sick.

This last point came up in *Estelle* v. *Gamble* (1976), when the Supreme Court declared that "deliberate indifference to the serious medical needs of prisoners constitutes unnecessary and wanton infliction of pain proscribed [forbidden] by the Eighth Amendment." The poor medical care was condemned as cruel and unusual punishment.

The issue of sentences *to* prison involves first of all the length of sentences in relation to the types of crimes committed. Some sentences may seem too long to some judicial bodies. One case involved more than thirty days in solitary confinement. When the case reached the Supreme Court (*Holt* v. *Jinney*, 1978), the justices agreed that thirty days should be the limit. Life sentences are often appealed as excessive for particular prisoners. The only other challenge is that life sentences should not be used at all. They might be condemned as cruel and unusual under the Eighth Amendment. So far, the Supreme Court has not been called on to deliver a ruling on that subject.

In making decisions according to the Eighth Amendment, the Supreme Court respects the authority of lower courts and state legislatures. Prison questions usually have been looked at many times before they reach our highest tribunal. There often are issues that should have been considered more fully at a lower level.

A case frequently referred to was decided by the Supreme Court in 1949. A convict who escaped from prison asked not to be returned. He said violence in the prison subjected him to cruel and unusual punishment. A lower court ruled that this prisoner was protected by the Eighth Amendment. It agreed that his appeal should be accepted. The Supreme Court disagreed. The justices explained their judgment on the ground that the prisoner had not appealed to all the state authorities who might have helped him.

The Meaning of Incorporation

The balance between the government of the United States and the states is the subject of incorporation. The Bill of Rights has always been interpreted as applying to the rights of Americans, protecting them from abuses by the national government. But do those ten amendments to the Constitution protect Americans from actions of their state governments? For example, the Eighth Amendment forbids cruel and unusual punishments meted out by federal courts. Does this prohibition extend to the state courts? Before the Civil War, this question would have been answered mostly with a loud no. Defenders of states' rights declared that the Constitution left to the states the protection of the individual's rights against actions of the states.

In the nineteenth century, the Supreme Court agreed. In *Barron* v. *Baltimore* (1833), the Court stated that the Fifth Amendment did not apply to the states. For instance, the right of defendants not to incriminate themselves applied only to the federal courts. Then came the Civil War and the end of slavery. This led to the Fourteenth Amendment (1868), which stated: "No State shall make or enforce any law which shall abridge the privileges or immunities of citizens of the United States, nor shall any State deprive any person of life, liberty, or property, without due process of law; nor deny to any person within its jurisdiction the equal protection of the laws."

The Fourteenth Amendment defended freedom in the states so widely that it seemed to many experts to incorporate (include) the Bill of Rights. They claimed that the due process of law clause in the Fourteenth Amendment enforced all the rights and freedoms in the first ten amendments. But opponents of incorporation argued that the Fourteenth Amendment did not apply to particular rights in the Bill of Rights. In *Walker* v. *Sauvinet* (1876), the Supreme Court declared that the trial by jury clause in the Seventh Amendment was not covered by the Fourteenth Amendment.

In *Near* v. *Minnesota* (1931), the Supreme Court said that the free press clause of the First Amendment applied to the states. Jay Near published a Minnesota newspaper that accused the state government of corruption. The paper was condemned by a state court as "malicious, scandalous and defamatory." Near was ordered to stop publication. The paper appealed to the Supreme Court, which supported the appeal. This was the first time the Court clearly defended incorporation of one of the rights in the Bill of Rights.

Another major case was *Palko* v. *Connecticut* (1937). The Supreme Court refused to incorporate the Fifth Amendment's double jeopardy clause, which forbids defendants to be tried twice for the same offense. However, Justice Benjamin N. Cardozo made an important statement on incorporation. His solution was to say that the Fourteenth Amendment incorporates part of the Bill of Rights, but not all of it. This was called *selective* incorporation. Cardozo said that the provisions of the Bill of Rights were incorporated where liberty and justice could not exist without them. The other provisions were not incorporated.

In contrast to selective incorporation is *total* incorporation, which Justice Hugo Black defended in a dissenting opinion in *Adamson* v. *California* (1947). Black wanted the whole Bill of Rights to be taken over and included in the Fourteenth Amendment. The majority on the Court did not agree with him. But the Court kept applying more clauses of the Bill of Rights to state actions according to the Cardozo doctrine of selective incorporation. In *Mapp* v. *Ohio* (1961), the Warren Court (1953–69), presided over by Chief Justice Earl Warren, began a process of incorporating whole sections of the Bill of Rights.

The justices considered the Eighth Amendment's protection against cruel and unusual punishments in *Robinson* v. *California* (1962). The Court ruled that the guarantee of protection against cruel and unusual punishments also applied to the states. Although that clause has been incorporated, that is not the case for protection against excessive bail and fines imposed at the state and local levels.

Why has the Supreme Court been so reluctant to accept total incorporation? The justices opposing it have usually said that the entire Bill of Rights should not be included in the Fourteenth Amendment because so many provisions are difficult to set down in clear terms. The justices have said that the most important provisions had to be dealt with, no matter how difficult they were. The others, like bail and fines, could be left for a future Supreme Court to deal with.

Other Claims to Cruel and Unusual Punishments

The Eighth Amendment and punishment in the public schools reached the Supreme Court in 1977. The issue was corporal punishment. It was decided in *Ingraham* v. *Wright*. The defendant, James Ingraham, was a pupil in a Florida school. He was paddled more than twenty times while held down on a table. He was also struck at other times, and as a result needed medical attention. Once he was unable to use his arm for a week.

In *Ingraham* v. *Wright*, the Supreme Court sustained, that is, upheld, a lower court in rejecting an appeal. The justices argued that the Eighth Amendment was intended by Madison to apply to adults only. For children, said the justices, the "openness of the public school and its supervision by the community afford significant safeguards against the kinds of abuses from which the Eighth Amendment protects the prisoners."

Sometimes rather unusual sentences are called cruel and unusual by defense lawyers. This occurred in 1990 in Nebraska. The case began as a rape accusation. It led to a sentence that the judge admitted was unique in his experience. Elizabeth Richardson made the charge of rape against Gary Nitsch. The fact was reported in newspapers and on radio. But no evidence to support her charge

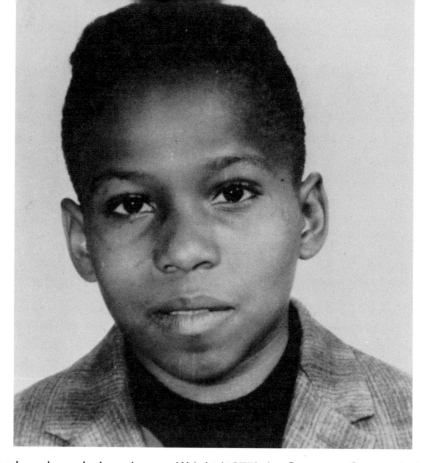

James Ingraham. In *Ingraham* v. *Wright* (1977) the Supreme Court ruled that the paddling Ingraham had received was not cruel and unusual punishment. According to the Court, such paddling was constitutional when used to maintain school discipline. However, students do have the right to sue if it is believed that the punishment is excessive.

could be found, and at last she confessed she made up the story. She pleaded "no contest" to a charge of perjury. This meant she did not say she was guilty, but she did give up her claim to be innocent.

Judge John Murphy sentenced Richardson to six months in jail. The judge also sentenced her to pay for advertisements, in newspapers and on radio, apologizing to Nitsch. The judge's reasoning went like this. Her charge against this man had been publicized in newspapers and on radio. So it was only fair to him that they should be used to publicize her apology.

Her lawyer said that she could appeal under three Amendments to the Constitution—the First, the Eighth, and the Fourteenth. Of course, the Eighth Amendment would be invoked under the cruel and unusual punishment clause.

The Eighth Amendment protects Americans against cruel and unusual punishments by the federal and state governments. But controversies about this clause continue to grow.

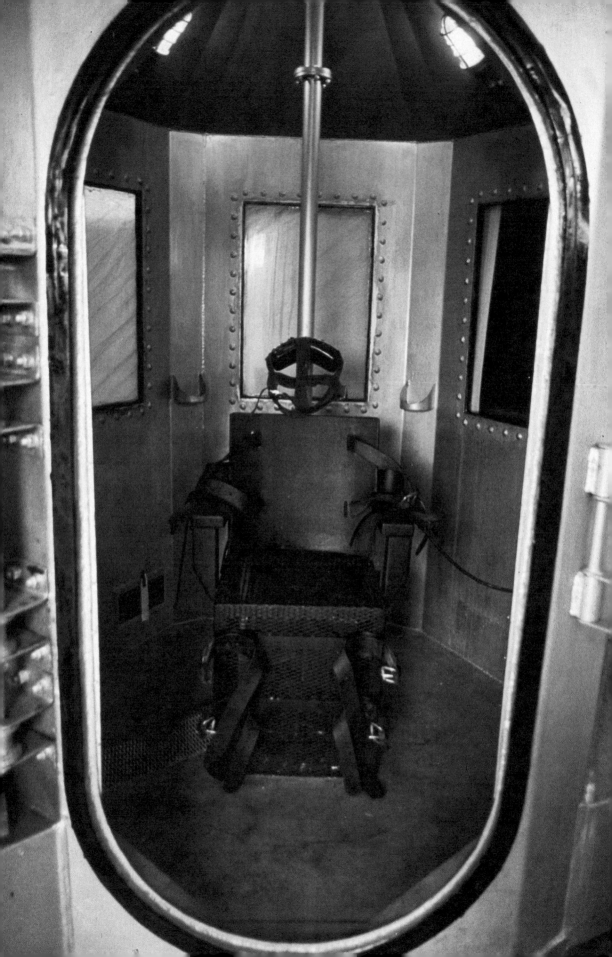

CHAPTER 5

The Death Penalty

"[T]he Eighth Amendment demands more than that a challenged punishment be acceptable to contemporary society. The Court also must ask whether it comports [fits in] with the basic concept of human dignity at the core of the Amendment."

JUSTICE POTTER STEWART, in *Gregg* v. *Georgia* (1976)

The ultimate punishment for criminals is the death penalty. All the fines and prisons are minor compared to the taking of a human life by the state. No other punishment is final and irreversible. Judges and juries, therefore, have an awesome responsibility when they sentence convicted criminals to capital punishment.

Kill a Criminal?

One of the main reasons for capital punishment has always been the belief that a human being who deliberately and coldbloodedly kills another human being deserves to die. Many other crimes have been punished by the death penalty, and some still are—for example, a plane hijacking in which somebody is killed. Yet, murder is the one crime that most people seem to believe merits capital punishment.

The Bible sanctions the ultimate penalty in Numbers 35.16: "The murderer shall surely be put to death." Throughout history the weight of opinion has been in favor of this punishment. Both the Greeks and the Romans used the death penalty for a long list of

---

The electric chair is used in several states to electrocute criminals. The Supreme Court has ruled that the death penalty is not cruel and unusual punishment.

crimes. Socrates, the Greek philosopher, was condemned on a charge of introducing new gods and corrupting the youth of Athens. The city authorities sentenced him to death, and he was forced to drink hemlock. That poison killed him. Cicero, the Roman writer and politician, was beheaded by his political enemies when his party lost power. Both Socrates and Cicero suffered cruel and unusual punishments by our standards.

Throughout history, the crime of treason—supporting the enemy or giving the enemy aid and comfort—has usually been punished by death. In the 1240s, England developed a method of executing traitors referred to as being hanged, drawn, and quartered. The traitor, tied to the tail of a horse or carried in a cart, was dragged to the gallows. The traitor was then hanged until he was half dead and then cut down. The executioner usually cut out the heart and held it up to view. Next, his intestines were cut out and burned. The traitor's head was then cut off and his body divided into quarters. Usually the head was displayed in a public place.

Murder has always been the crime that most clearly called for the death of the criminal. Sometimes murder has been linked to other crimes. Thus, the murder of a public figure because he or she *is* a public figure is assassination. The murder of someone held against his or her will involves not only murder but kidnapping.

A famous case from early modern history was the assassination of Henry IV, king of France, in 1610. His murderer was executed after barbarous torture. The suffering of the assassin disgusted some leaders of French public opinion, and their criticism contributed to the growing feeling that torture should not be used, even with the worst criminals.

The United States has had four presidents murdered. James A. Garfield was assassinated by Charles Guiteau in 1881, and William McKinley was assassinated by Leon Czolgosz in 1901. In each case, the assassin was executed. Abraham Lincoln's assassin, John Wilkes Booth, was never sentenced because he was killed trying to escape in 1865. The alleged assassin of John F. Kennedy, Lee Harvey Oswald, was never sentenced because he himself was murdered shortly after his arrest.

Kidnapping is associated for most people with the Lindbergh case. The Lindbergh Law was passed by Congress as a result of this case. The infant son of Charles Lindbergh, the first aviator to fly across the Atlantic by himself, was kidnapped in 1932. The baby was later found dead. A German immigrant named Bruno Richard Hauptmann was charged with the crime and was found guilty. He was executed in the electric chair. Congress passed the Lindbergh Law, making kidnapping a federal offense if the victim was taken out of state. The law also stated that a kidnapper could be executed if the victim was not released unharmed.

Many humanitarians have accepted the death penalty as an unfortunate necessity. Writing in 1776, Thomas Jefferson said that it "should be the last melancholy resource against those whose existence is become inconsistent with the safety of their fellow citizens."

Jefferson preferred to see criminals reformed and restored to society as useful citizens. But he agreed that there were incorrigibles—those who could not be reformed. He held that those who had committed murder, and might do so again, had given up their right to life. They had to be removed from society permanently.

When James Madison wrote the Bill of Rights, he allowed for capital punishment. The Fifth Amendment uses the phrase "a capital, or otherwise infamous [unforgivable] crime." The term *capital crime* refers to a serious crime that may lead to the death penalty. Madison's purpose was to surround it with protections to make sure the criminal was treated justly.

Nearly two centuries later, Chief Justice Warren Burger made the logical connection between the Fifth and Eighth Amendments: "Since the Eighth Amendment was adopted on the same day in 1791 as the Fifth Amendment, it hardly needs more to establish that the death penalty was not 'cruel' in the constitutional sense at that time."

There are three reasons supporters of capital punishment give for keeping the death penalty. First, there is retribution—a punishment for a crime. The criminal pays with his or her life for taking somebody else's. Second, there is deterrence—the discouragement of similar action. Those who might commit murder are stopped by the fear of execution. Third, there is protection for society. The executed criminal cannot commit murder again.

There is a strong movement against the death penalty. It includes lawyers, criminologists, and other concerned citizens. Opponents of the death penalty point to a number of arguments. There is the danger that innocent people will be executed. This is known to have happened when false evidence sent defendants to their death. According to a 1987 study, 350 people convicted of murder since the beginning of this century were innocent. Twenty-three of them were executed. James Richmond of Arcadia, Florida, nearly joined their number in 1988. After being convicted of murder, Richardson spent more than twenty years on death row, as the prison area housing inmates sentenced to death is usually called. Richmond was close to his execution when he was saved by new evidence that showed he did not commit the crime. A terrible mistake was barely avoided.

Another argument against capital punishment is that it does not decrease the murder rate and may even increase it. Studies over the past hundred years have provided no evidence that capital punishment reduces the rate of murder. Whereas some would-be murderers might be deterred by fear of the death penalty, other persons may commit murder because of the death penalty. They may do so to experience the thrill of taking a chance on death. Or they may be unbalanced people who commit murder in the hope of being executed. Whatever the motive, according to this argument, ordinary citizens are more likely to be murdered because of the death penalty.

Another argument against capital punishment is that ordinary citizens may become accustomed to violent death when they see their government officials subjecting criminals to violent death. These citizens may be led into accepting all kinds of violent acts that they would normally oppose.

The argument about retribution (the criminal gets what he or she deserves) is answered by saying that no criminal deserves the horrors of death row followed by execution. It is inhuman, say the critics, to make any human being go through such horrors.

Many state courts have stopped imposing the death penalty. Thirteen state legislatures followed the lead offered by Maine, which abolished the death penalty in 1887. All the other states have drastically limited the kinds of crimes that call for capital punishment. Armed robbery and espionage (spying) are examples of crimes that are now punished by prison sentences but not the death penalty. In *Coker* v. *Georgia* (1977), the Supreme Court overruled the death penalty for rape of an adult woman that did not result in her death.

Murder remains as the major crime for which the death penalty may be imposed. The Supreme Court has never declared the death penalty itself to be a cruel and unusual punishment under the Eighth Amendment. Many of the arguments about the death penalty have been about the manner in which it is imposed and carried out.

Methods of Execution

The Supreme Court made an important distinction about cruelty in 1949: "The cruelty against which the Constitution protects a guilty man is cruelty inherent in [belong to] the method of punishment, not the necessary suffering involved in any method humanely employed to extinguish life humanely."

What type of execution should be used in carrying out the death sentences imposed by judges or juries? A number of types have been tried in the United States in recent years. All have produced horrible cases in which the execution was not humane.

Hanging had been the preferred method of execution for centuries. It has been the subject of horror stories. Grim jokes became known as "gallows humor" in eighteenth-century England and America. The reference was to the gallows, the wooden structure on which hangings took place. Many times the trap door of the gallows failed to open and left the condemned person waiting for it to be fixed. Other times the trap door opened too soon, and the condemned person plunged downward before the rope was properly adjusted around his or her neck. The rope has been known to break. At times, it has been so long that the condemned person landed on the ground or so short as to cause death by prolonged choking.

Most executions by hanging have been carried out skillfully and professionally. The real debate is against hanging as such. According to its opponents, breaking a victim's neck is a horrible way to kill anyone and should be abolished.

Only two states now permit execution by hanging. Agreeing that hanging was too cruel, many states turned to electrocution. The electric chair was widely adopted in the early twentieth century. Its defenders argued that putting the condemned person in a chair wired to carry high-voltage electricity, and then sending lethal jolts through the wires, was a more humane method of execution. The electric chair was thought to kill so quickly as to be almost painless. This has not always been so.

The case of *Louisiana ex rel. Francis* v. *Resweber* reached the Supreme Court in 1947. The defendant survived the high voltage of the electric chair. The mechanism hadn't worked. He was returned to death row, and a new date was set for his execution. Francis appealed to the Supreme Court, claiming that the strain of being forced to undergo the process again was cruel and unusual punishment, even if officials had not intended it to be so. In a 5-to-4 majority decision, the Court said that executing him would not be cruel and unusual punishment since there was "no purpose to inflict unnecessary pain." Four of the justices dissented. They said that the *intent* of the executioner didn't matter as far as the issue of cruel and unusual punishment went. They protested what they called "death by installment." Francis was taken back to the electric chair. This time he died in it.

When Jesse Tafero was electrocuted in Florida in 1990, it took three jolts to kill him. He was a frightful sight with flames burning the mask over his head. Thirteen states now provide electrocution as the method of execution.

The gas chamber seemed a better alternative to some state authorities. The usual method is to strap the condemned person into a chair in a padded room and then pump a lethal dose of potassium chloride into the room. This gas is supposed to be inhaled like air. The victim is supposed to die without feeling anything. But, in truth, this has not always been a painless method of execution. Those in the padded room have been known to resist the poison gas. Their lungs have struggled to expel it. The result has been the spectacle of condemned persons choking for several minutes before subsiding into death. Many spectators—prison officials, state authorities, even executioners themselves—have stated that the use of the gas chamber is too cruel and should be stopped.

Four states continue to provide lethal gas methods of execution.

Then there is lethal injection. When first introduced, it was said to be the most nearly painless method of execution. Its defenders said the executioner's needle would cause no more pain than a

A death chamber where criminals sentenced to death are given a lethal injection. Twenty states use lethal injection as a means of killing prisoners sentenced to death.

doctor's injection to cause unconsciousness. After lethal injection had been tried in many cases, the method came under fire. Critics argued that doctors sometimes have trouble finding the right vein for an injection and that some executioners were having the same trouble. When Raymond Landry was put to death in Texas in 1989, the executioner could not find the right vein at the first attempt. He tried again and again, while the victim winced and shuddered at the pain of the needle entering his arm. More than half an hour passed before a lethal injection took hold and killed him. The condemned man suffered physically and psychologically. Those who watched were appalled. Twenty states provide lethal injection methods.

Utah retains shooting as its method of taking a criminal's life. This is an old tradition. Almost as soon as the gun was invented, it was used in executions. The firing squad became a fixture in killing criminals. A French firing squad shot Mata Hari, a woman condemned as a spy for the Germans during World War I. This method has always been a favorite with the military, which considered it more dignified than hanging. But there is always the possibility that a volley of bullets from the rifles of a firing squad will fail to kill the condemned criminal. In *Wilkerson* v. *Utah* (1878) the Supreme Court approved execution by firing squad. The Court has never reversed that ruling.

Death Row

Execution is not the only suffering of those condemned to death. There is also the mental suffering between conviction and sentencing and execution. The period on death row can be absolute hell for prisoners. Psychologists have studied their reactions. Official reports show that some prisoners withdraw into themselves, lose touch with reality, and suffer from hallucinations. Others suffer from delusions that they are free. Still others go insane. And suicide is common where it is possible.

A long time on death row has a lot to do with these psychopathic seizures. Prisoners often spend years while their lawyers are making appeals. The appeals process for capital punishment cases now averages eight years. It is a terrible experience.

A century ago, in 1889, the Supreme Court noted the problem after the final verdict is given:

> When a prisoner sentenced by a court to death is confined in the penitentiary awaiting the execution of his sentence, one of the most horrible feelings to which he can be subjected during that time is the uncertainty during the whole of it, which may exist for a period of four weeks, as to the precise time when his execution shall take place.

Unbearable tension develops when the fate of an appeal is unknown. Will the governor call off the execution? This has sometimes happened only hours before an execution was scheduled. Meanwhile, the convict watches fearfully as the clock ticks away. Much worse are the dreadful cases when the stay of execution arrives too late, after the execution.

At least the surroundings and atmosphere in which executions take place is better than in former times. Public executions used to be the rule. It was thought that the sight of a murderer losing his or her life would frighten others away from committing the same crime. However, these occasions too often turned into a circuslike atmosphere. Morbid crowds came as if they were attending an acrobatic performance or a prize fight. The convict on the gallows became the object of jokes and laughter. As a result, the states stopped holding public executions. Today only a few people (mainly state and prison officials) are allowed to see the condemned die.

For the Framers of the Constitution and the Bill of Rights, the death penalty was an accepted sentence for many crimes. In the twentieth century, the use of the death penalty in the United States has declined, but not the controversy that surrounds it.

Court Controversies

"[T]he infliction of death as a punishment for murder is not without justification and thus is not unconstitutionally severe."

JUSTICE POTTER STEWART, the majority opinion in
Gregg v. *Georgia* (1976)

"The death penalty, unnecessary to promote the goal of deterrence or to further any legitimate notion of retribution, is an excessive penalty forbidden by the Eighth and Fourteenth Amendments. I respectfully dissent from the Court's judgment upholding the sentences of death."

JUSTICE THURGOOD MARSHALL, dissenting in
Gregg v. *Georgia* (1976)

Controversy over the death penalty has grown steadily since the 1970s. In recent years about 22,000 people per year have been arrested for murder. In many cases, no suspect has been arrested. In the early 1990s, more than 2,200 convicted criminals were under sentence of death. As many of them appeal their cases, the court controversies continue.

Arguments Over the Death Sentence

During the 1970s, the Supreme Court decided several very important cases dealing with capital punishment. The most important of these cases were *Furman* v. *Georgia* (1972) and *Gregg* v. *Georgia* (1976).

Justice William J. Brennan, Jr., served on the Supreme Court from 1956 to 1987. In a dissenting opinion in *Gregg* v. *Georgia* (1976), he expressed his viewpoint that the death penalty "for whatever crime and under all circumstances, is 'cruel and unusual' in violation of the Eighth and Fourteenth Amendment of the Constitution."

Charlie Furman was a burglar who entered a home in the middle of the night. The owner of the house found him, and Furman attempted to flee. The burglar tripped. The gun he was carrying went off, killing the owner. Furman was captured, tried for murder, and sentenced to death. His appeal went up through the courts in Georgia and finally reached the Supreme Court.

Two other cases, *Jackson* v. *Georgia* and *Branch* v. *Texas*, were considered by the Court at the same time. The basic argument of those appealing their sentences was this: The standards of decency had evolved, that is, developed, to the point in American history where capital punishment could no longer be tolerated. All three posed a common question: Would the death penalty in these cases be cruel and unusual punishment in the Eighth Amendment sense?

By a majority of 5 to 4, the Supreme Court ruled in *Furman* v. *Georgia* (1972) that the death penalty *as it was then imposed under certain state laws* was cruel and unusual punishment and so violated the Eighth Amendment. The Court found the basic problems to be that the sentencing authorities (jury and judge) had not been given specific legal guidelines for making their decisions. They had not been directed to give attention to the circumstances surrounding the crime. Nor did they give attention to the character or record of the defendant.

Each of the five justices who supported the majority decision gave a different reason for his position.

The problems were complex. No wonder this was the longest written case in the history of the Supreme Court.

Justice William O. Douglas was one of those who supported the majority opinion:

The high service rendered [given] by the "cruel and unusual" punishment clause of the Eighth Amendment is to require legislatures to write penal laws [laws about punishment] that are even-handed, nonselective, and nonarbitrary [not based on whim], and to see to it that general laws are not applied sparsely, selectively, and spottily to unpopular groups.

According to Douglas, the juries that set the death penalty were allowed too much freedom to decide between punishments. They did it without protections against prejudice and whim in making up their minds. Douglas was against the death penalty in these cases.

Justice William Brennan opposed the death penalty under any circumstances. He did not want it *ever* to be carried out. He wrote that "a punishment must not by its severity be degrading to human dignity." He felt that capital punishment was degrading to human dignity. Justice Brennan naturally opposed the death penalty in the cases before him.

Justice Thurgood Marshall agreed with Brennan that the death penalty should be outlawed completely. He gave two reasons. First, he considered the death penalty excessive. Second, he wrote that if the American people had the facts about the death penalty they would find it morally unacceptable. In addition, he noted that the death penalty falls on the poor and minorities more than on others.

Justice Potter Stewart opposed the death penalty sentences under consideration in *Furman* v. *Georgia* (1972) because they were "so wantonly and so freakishly imposed," that is, with no just or consistent reasoning.

Justice Byron White said that the state legislatures did not provide sufficient control over judges and juries in capital cases.

These five justices made up the majority in *Furman* v. *Georgia*. They held that the death penalty, as imposed, was cruel and unusual punishment. The minority of four was led by Chief Justice Warren E. Burger. He wrote a dissenting opinion that favored the death penalty in this case: Burger defended capital punishment by referring to history: "In the 181 years since the enactment of the Eighth Amendment, not a single decision of this Court has cast the slightest shadow of a doubt on the constitutionality of capital punishment." Burger defended the right of juries to set the death penalty. He argued that no system can be perfectly consistent. Differences in jury verdicts do not prove that the jury system of arriving at verdicts is a bad one.

Justices Harry A. Blackmun, Lewis F. Powell, Jr., and William H. Rehnquist also dissented from the majority. All four dissenters believed that if the death penalty were to be abolished, it should be done by a law, not by a judicial decision.

The death sentences under consideration in *Furman* v. *Georgia* were overturned. So were hundreds of others that were covered by the ruling. That was because the Court had ruled that trial and sentencing procedures needed to be changed. New procedures would make sure that there no longer was a great risk that the death penalty would be decided in an unfair manner.

Opponents of the death penalty hoped that the ruling in *Furman* v. *Georgia* (1972) would lead to the success of their campaign to end capital punishment. They looked forward to a future case in which the Supreme Court would declare executions to be forbidden by the Eighth Amendment. After all, two members of the Court, Justices Marshall and Brennan, were already against the death penalty in all cases. Perhaps other justices or new justices would join them.

Supporters of the death penalty took a different view. They were encouraged by the fact that only the conditions surrounding the trials and sentencing had been questioned by most of the justices in *Furman* v. *Georgia*—not the death penalty itself. For them, the problem was to change the conditions. State legislatures did this by passing new laws governing judges and juries in cases involving capital punishment. These laws were intended to correct the problems criticized by the Supreme Court.

A typical solution for the states was to divide trials into two stages. During the first stage, the verdict—the judgment whether the defendant is guilty or not guilty—would be decided. If the defendant was found guilty, then the legal process would go on. The second stage concerned the sentence: Was the criminal to be condemned to death?

College students at a pro-death-penalty demonstration. Recent polls have shown that about 75 percent of Americans support the death penalty for certain crimes.

After the verdict of guilty was made known *but before the sentence was pronounced,* defense lawyers were to be allowed to present all the evidence they had in favor of their clients. This might include what are called mitigating circumstances. These are the facts or events surrounding the crime that, while not an excuse for the crime, may be considered in fairness and mercy as reducing the amount of moral blame. For example, if a criminal came from a broken home, that fact would be taken into account.

The prosecuting attorney would be allowed to present negative information about the criminal. Such aggravating circumstances, as they are called, could include facts and events surrounding the crime and would make it seem worse. An example might be the fact that the murderer beat and tortured the victim before killing him or her. In some cases, juries were given the power to make the final decision about the sentence. With the new information provided to them, these juries were thought to have enough information to make a careful, reasonable judgment. These juries are called informed juries.

In other states, sentences were mandated, that is, required. Laws were passed directly connecting specific types of crimes with specific sentences. Juries were not given a choice of sentences to choose from. Juries were told that if they found a defendant guilty of murder in the first degree *then they had to pass a death sentence.* Since the sentence would be the same for all people guilty of this crime, the states believed no one could claim that different defendants were being treated differently.

Thirty-five states wrote new laws dealing with informed juries, mandated sentences, and other procedures in the sentencing process. The purpose of the new laws was to meet the Supreme Court's demands that death sentences not be imposed "wantonly and . . . freakishly."

For example, the newly written Georgia laws allowed the death penalty for six kinds of crimes: murder, kidnapping for ransom or where the victim is harmed, armed robbery, rape, treason, and aircraft hijacking. The new Georgia law provided for the two-step procedure: first determining guilt or innocence, then sentencing. Before a convicted criminal could be sentenced to death, at least one out of a list of ten specific kinds of aggravating circumstances had to be found "beyond a reasonable doubt." Among these specific aggravating circumstances were the following: The criminal had a previous record of serious crimes. The criminal committed the murder for the purpose of receiving money. The crime was particularly vile and horrible because it involved torture. As a further limit on the sentencing, if the court decided on the death penalty, it had to refer to similar cases. The reason for this was to show that the particular death sentence was not excessive or disproportionate to penalties handed out in similar cases.

The Death Penalty Is Constitutional

The Supreme Court's next big ruling on capital punishment was in *Gregg* v. *Georgia* (1976). Troy Gregg was a hitchhiker in Georgia. He was picked up by two men and given a ride. The two men were found dead. Gregg was arrested. The charge against him stated that he had murdered and robbed the two men. A jury found Gregg guilty of murder and armed robbery. At the sentencing stage, the jury decided on the death sentence. His case finally ended up in the Supreme Court. By a majority of 7 to 2, the Court ruled that the new state laws under which Gregg was sentenced to death did not violate the Constitution.

Justice Potter Stewart, writing the majority opinion in *Gregg* v. *Georgia* (1976), declared that the new Georgia laws corrected the abuses pointed out in *Furman* v. *Georgia* (1972): "No longer can a jury wantonly and freakishly impose the death sentence." The Supreme Court majority agreed that the sentence of death had not resulted from prejudice and was not excessive. Justice Stewart wrote that "the infliction of death as a punishment for murder is not without justification and thus is not unconstitutionally severe."

The two dissenters in the case were Justices Brennan and Marshall. They still opposed capital punishment at all times, not just in circumstances surrounding particular cases.

In his dissenting opinion in *Gregg* v. *Georgia* (1976), Justice Brennan repeated part of his opinion given in *Furman* v. *Georgia* (1972). He held that since executions "degrade human dignity" they are ruled out by the Eighth Amendment:

This Court . . . has the duty . . . to say whether . . . "moral concepts" require us to hold that the law has progressed to the point where we should declare that the punishment of death, like punishments on the rack, the screw and the wheel, is no longer morally tolerable in our civilized society.

In his dissenting opinion, Justice Marshall focused on two arguments supporters of capital punishment used: deterrence and retribution. With regard to deterrence, Marshall wrote that there was no proof that executions lowered the murder rate. There was no available evidence to prove that the fear of execution frightened would-be murderers. With regard to retribution, Marshall did not accept the argument that a murderer deserved to pay with his or her life for taking a life. Marshall opposed capital punishment because it "has as its very basis the total denial of the wrong-doer's dignity and worth." Marshall felt that life in prison, not execution, would be the proper sentence.

During the same year, the Supreme Court ruled on the question of whether mandatory death sentences were constitutional. In a 5 to 4 decision, the Supreme Court ruled in *Roberts* v. *Louisiana I* (1976) that mandatory death penalty laws that require the death

Protestors demonstrate against the death penalty. In the landmark *Gregg* case (1976), two of the nine justices voted against the death penalty.

penalty for every defendant convicted of murder are unconstitutional. The next year in *Roberts* v. *Louisiana II* (1977), the Court ruled unconstitutional the Louisiana law even if that law mandated the death penalty only for the killing of a firefighter or police officer. The reason for overturning the state law was this: By requiring the death sentence, the law had not allowed "for consideration of whatever mitigating circumstances may be relevant to either the particular offender or the particular offense." Required death sentences were rejected by the Court as cruel and unusual punishment under the Eighth Amendment.

The issue of imposing the death penalty for crimes that did not involve murder soon came up. *Coker* v. *Georgia* (1977) was a rape case involving the death sentence. During an armed robbery, the defendant had raped an adult woman. He was sentenced to death by a Georgia court. The case was eventually appealed to the Supreme Court. In a 7-to-2 decision, the Court ruled that the death penalty in this case was cruel and unusual punishment because the victim was not a minor and because she survived the attack. It was also pointed out that Georgia was the only state that allowed the death penalty for rape. In addition, in the previous four years Georgia juries had not imposed the death sentence in 90 percent of rape convictions.

During the 1970s, the Supreme Court set better guidelines to keep death sentences from violating the rights of the accused. But it also declared that death sentences were constitutional, and therefore could be justly imposed as long as the rights of the accused were protected. The Court therefore left open some questions about capital punishment.

During the 1980s, the Court reviewed a number of cases that helped to clarify the rules governing the death penalty. In *Ford* v. *Wainwright* (1986), the Supreme Court decided against the execution of criminals who became, and remained, insane on death row.

In *Sumner* v. *Shuman* (1987), the Court ruled 6 to 3 that the death penalty cannot be required when prisoners serving life sentences murder other prisoners or prison guards. The Court held that, since some murders in prison are worse than others, different punishments may be imposed in different cases. The Court stated that the death penalty may be justified but the jury had to be persuaded—not forced—to impose a death sentence.

This was an important ruling because many people, including some prison officials, fear the consequences if life termers are not frightened by fear of execution. Life in prison, according to the argument, is the worst that can happen when death is forbidden. Life termers might commit murder because they know that nothing worse than imprisonment can happen to them.

Another question that the Supreme Court recently reviewed is the constitutionality of executing mentally retarded convicted murderers. Experts estimate that somewhere between 10 and 30 percent of the criminals on death row are mentally retarded. Johnny Paul Penry was convicted of a brutal murder. He had raped, beaten, and stabbed his victim. Penry was mentally retarded. He suffered brain damage either from birth or from severe beatings he had received early in his childhood. He had the mental age of a six- or seven-year-old. The Supreme Court in *Penry* v. *Lynaugh* (1989) upheld Penry's death sentence. The Eighth Amendment did not prohibit his execution, the Court said, since mental retardation may not prevent someone from knowing right from wrong.

As previously discussed, death sentences may be affected by aggravating or mitigating circumstances. Aggravating circumstances are those that may make a crime seem worse, as when murderers beat their victims before killing them. Mitigating circumstances are those that may make a crime seem less evil, as when murderers come from broken homes. The Supreme Court held in *Blystone* v. *Pennsylvania* (1990) that the death penalty is acceptable for those convicted of capital crimes if there is at least one aggravating circumstance and no mitigating circumstances. The Court held in *McKoy* v. *North Carolina* (1990) that the state was wrong in preventing jurors from considering mitigating circumstances unless all the jurors agree that mitigating circumstances exist.

Another factor affecting capital punishment is the attitude of convicted prisoners. Some confess their crimes and are known to be guilty from that fact alone. Others claim to be innocent throughout their time in court and on death row. These prisoners usually receive a favorable hearing because of the belief that they might be telling the truth. That belief creates a fear that an innocent person might be executed.

Capital punishment is a complicated subject. It involves many factors including legal and moral issues. Some cases have both aggravating and mitigating circumstances. These are some of the reasons capital punishment is such a difficult problem for the courts, including the Supreme Court.

CHAPTER 7

Unfair Sentences

"First and last, people are sent to jail because they are poor."

CLARENCE DARROW

The Sixth Amendment guarantees the right of all defendants in criminal cases to a speedy and public trial by an impartial jury. The Eighth Amendment supports this right when it forbids cruel and unusual punishments. Such punishments may come about because defendants have not been given a fair trial.

Juries and the Death Penalty

Racial, religious, and ethnic prejudice can influence a juror's or judge's decisions. The Supreme Court has condemned such prejudice as a circumstance that causes unfair sentences. In *Furman* v. *Georgia* (1972), the death penalty was reversed partly because those who imposed it were prejudiced against the defendant.

Justice William O. Douglas spoke eloquently about prejudice leading to cruel and unusual punishments:

Chief Justice William H. Rehnquist served as an associate justice on the Supreme Court from 1972 to 1986. Since then, he has been chief justice. In the majority opinion in *Lockhart* v. *McCree,* Rehnquist stated that the Constitution does not prohibit keeping off juries in possible death-penalty cases those who are absolutely opposed to the death sentence.

In a Nation committed to equal protection of the laws there is no permissible "caste" aspect of law enforcement. Yet we know that the discretion [freedom] of judges and juries in imposing the death penalty enables the penalty to be selectively applied, feeding prejudices against the accused if he is poor and despised, lacking in political clout, or if he is a member of a suspect or unpopular minority, and saving those who by social position may be in a more protected position.

Douglas noted that trials can be influenced by the wealth or poverty of those on trial. Defendants with money can afford to hire the best trial lawyers, who will present their cases effectively in court. Defendants without money may have to rely on court-appointed lawyers. These lawyers may be ill-paid, overworked, and unfamiliar with the details of their cases. If so, they cannot represent their clients effectively. A rich defendant may get a lenient sentence when a poor defendant gets a harsh sentence. Indeed, the two sentences may be, literally, a matter of life and death—prison for one, execution for the other.

Court procedures came under examination in many cases because of prejudice in sentencing. Sometimes this came about because of what are called scrupled jurors. A scrupled juror is one opposed to capital punishment as a matter of conscience. He or she has scruples against it. Scruples are ethical principles that discourage a particular action—in this case, scruples against supporting the death penalty. Such jurors are often excluded from juries by prosecuting attorneys, the lawyers who present cases against the accused in court. They want the death penalty to remain a possibility, so they challenge the right of scrupled jurors to sit on juries in capital cases. Their argument is that all jurors should be willing to consider all punishments, including the death penalty. One scrupled juror would make it impossible for a jury to sentence a convicted murderer to death. Therefore, according to this argument, such a scrupled juror should be excluded.

Critics of exclusion argue that keeping out scrupled jurors leads to "hanging juries." If all jurors on a jury are in favor of capital punishment, then the defendant is more likely to be found guilty and sentenced to death. Critics also point out that the Sixth Amendment protects the right to an impartial jury. In addition, the Court has repeatedly ruled that juries must represent a cross section of the community.

The question of scrupled jurors on juries came before the Supreme Court in *Witherspoon* v. *Illinois* (1968) and *Lockhart* v. *McCree* (1986). Here was the dilemma: Allowing scrupled jurors on a jury meant no death penalty. Forbidding scrupled jurors meant a real possibility of the death penalty. The Supreme Court at first got around the dilemma by making careful distinctions. Its ruling in *Witherspoon* v. *Illinois* (1968) amounted to this: The Court said that jurors completely and absolutely opposed to the death penalty were not the issue in this particular case. But jurors who disliked the death penalty but who would not oppose it at all times were. The Court ruled that jurors who dislike the death penalty may *not* be excluded from the sentencing part of the two-step trial process. Such jurors could not be rejected if they express a willingness to consider the death penalty as a possibility after examining the evidence. In other words, as long as capital punishment is constitutional, jurors who would prefer not to vote for the death penalty, but who *might*, would be regarded as impartial. They could sit on sentencing juries in cases that might lead to the death penalty.

People who were hesitant about the death penalty were not allowed to be jurors in the *Witherspoon* case. Therefore, the Supreme Court prohibited the death sentence in that case. But that decision still left open another question: Could persons definitely opposed to the death penalty in all circumstances be kept off juries that determine both the possible guilt of the accused and later the sentence of the convicted defendant?

That issue came up in 1986. McCree was going to be tried for murder. The judge prevented from serving on the jury anyone who definitely opposed the death penalty under all circumstances. The jury found McCree guilty of murder. It then sentenced him to life imprisonment without parole. (Parole is early release from prison so that the prisoner can serve the rest of his or her term outside prison.) McCree appealed the decision. He claimed that he had been denied his constitutional right to an impartial jury selected from a representative cross section of the community. When the case was appealed to a U.S. district court, it agreed with him. So did a U.S. court of appeals when the case was appealed to it. However, when the government appealed the case to the U.S. Supreme Court, the justices decided 6 to 3 against McCree's position.

Justice William H. Rehnquist presented the majority in *Lockhart* v. *McCree* (1986):

> Does the Constitution prohibit the removal for cause, prior to the guilt phase of a bifurcated [two-step] capital trial, of prospective [possible] jurors whose opposition to the death penalty is so strong that it would prevent or substantially impair the performance of their duties as jurors at the sentencing phase of the trial? . . . We hold that it does not.

In other words, those absolutely opposed to the death penalty can be kept from serving on juries that decide both the guilt and the sentencing in cases that could involve the death penalty.

Prejudice Against Minorities and Women

The worst prejudice in sentencing has almost always involved minorities. African Americans, Hispanic Americans, homosexuals, political radicals, and other groups have at times found themselves being unfairly treated in court. For example, although African Americans make up about 12 percent of the population of the United States, they make up about 40 percent of the people in prison. This is partly because of the United States's failure to achieve full equality of opportunity. Crime is common amid the poverty and helplessness of big city ghettos. The number of criminals produced in such environments is much higher than the

Justice Thurgood Marshall has served on the Supreme Court since 1967. He has opposed the death penalty in a number of Supreme Court cases.

average. White bias is also partly responsible. White judges and juries often draw on their own experiences in punishing crimes. Some studies of discrimination have shown that they are more likely to sentence defendants who are not white to longer terms or to death. However, other recent studies show that blacks and whites received generally similar sentences when two factors are taken into account: the seriousness of the crime and the sentencing practices of the state where the crime took place.

The civil rights movement of the 1950s and 1960s created massive changes in American society. One of the most important changes concerned the law and the courts. Thurgood Marshall was a leader in this field. As chief lawyer for the National Association for the Advancement of Colored People (NAACP), Marshall argued the case of *Brown* v. *Board of Education of Topeka* (1954) before the Supreme Court. It was a landmark case for the nation and a personal triumph for Marshall. The justices ruled that racial segregation in the public schools should cease. Marshall was appointed to the Supreme Court in 1967. The NAACP has continued to be one of the most active organizations in the fight for legal justice. It has been helpful in reducing the number of race-motivated sentences.

Other minorities—and women—have used similar organizing techniques and have worked to make sure that jury selection does not discriminate against them.

Political radicals holding unpopular opinions have also learned what it means to stand in a hostile courtroom. This happened to the leaders of a labor protest in Chicago in 1886. Workers had been demanding an eight-hour workday. A worker had been killed during a clash between the workers and police outside a factory. The next day strikers held a mass meeting in Haymarket Square. Their leaders attacked the policies of company executives. The police ordered the meeting to break up. Somebody threw a bomb, killing several policemen. The police then opened fire on the crowd. About seventy people were injured in the riot. The bomb thrower was never found. But the radical leaders were arrested, tried, and found guilty. Some were sentenced to death, others to long prison terms. Four were hanged in 1887.

In 1893, the new governor of Illinois, John Peter Altgeld, pardoned the surviving convicted men. His reason—the defendants were tried by a judge and jury inflamed by hatred for them (all but one of the radicals were German-speaking) and for their unpopular political beliefs. The sentences were unfair, and so the governor issued the pardons. He regretted that he could not have saved the executed, which he would have done because he opposed the death penalty.

The *Sacco-Vanzetti* case in Massachusetts is still debated. Nicola Sacco and Bartolomeo Vanzetti were Italian-born political

The murder trials resulting from the Haymarket Riot resulted in the conviction of political radicals, most of whom were German-speaking. The controversy over their conviction led the Illinois governor to pardon those who had not already been executed.

radicals. They were accused of killing a paymaster and a guard in a holdup in 1920. They were tried for murder and armed robbery and sentenced to death in 1921. Sacco and Vanzetti were convicted and sentenced by a court prejudiced against them. Many people believed that there was not much evidence and that they had been found guilty because of their ethnic background and their political beliefs. During the 1920s there were mass demonstrations in the United States, Latin America, and Europe, protesting what was regarded as an unfair trial. Despite the protests and controversy, in 1927 Sacco and Vanzetti were put to death by electrocution.

With women, different problems with prejudice have been common. Studies show that women commit about 13 percent of all

"The Passion of Sacco and Vanzetti" by Ben Shahn. Sacco and Vanzetti were the center of controversy in the 1920s when they were tried for and convicted of murder.

murders in the United States. But juries and judges are less likely to sentence women than men to death. The remedy for this has yet to be found. Another problem was not settled until 1975. Until that time, many states had rules that limited the number of women being selected for the groups from which jury members were selected. In *Taylor* v. *Louisiana* (1975), the Supreme Court ruled that the Sixth and Fourteenth Amendments did not allow states to have jury selection systems that excluded most women from jury service. With women serving on more juries, it cannot be claimed that death penalties have been arrived at because of unfair exclusion of women from juries.

How Old Is Old Enough?

Age causes special problems regarding unfair sentences. Some juveniles commit dreadful crimes. When they do, should they be subject to the death penalty? Some of those who answer yes say anyone old enough to commit a crime is old enough to pay for it. Others maintain that the rule of law must be enforced equally for all people no matter what their age.

Those who answer no say defendants under eighteen are too young to fully understand what they are doing. Some also say that juveniles are young enough to be reformed and returned to society. That is better, they believe, than removing young criminals from society by killing them.

The case of James Roach in South Carolina raised a peculiar problem. What if the crime was committed by a juvenile who lived to be an adult before his execution? Roach was convicted of the rape and murder of two teenage girls when he was seventeen. He was twenty-five when he was executed in 1986. The *Roach* case involved many controversial matters, including the eight years he spent on death row. Some might consider that to be cruel and unusual punishment. But Roach's age was what really angered reformers opposed to the death penalty. The Supreme Court did not intervene to save him.

The controversy about capital punishment of minors came up again in *Thompson* v. *Oklahoma* (1988). The defendant was fifteen years old when he took part with three others in a brutal murder. The victim was beaten, shot twice, cut in the throat, chest, and abdomen, chained to a concrete block, and thrown in a river. The four participants in this murder were tried separately and were sentenced to death. Thompson's case reached the Supreme Court because of his age. The Court ruled 5 to 3 against the sentence. The defendant was not executed.

Justice John P. Stevens wrote the majority opinion for *Thompson* v. *Oklahoma* (1988):

> The conclusion that it would offend civilized standards of decency to execute a person who was less than 16 years old at the time of his or her offense is consistent with the views that have been expressed by respected professional organizations, by other nations that share our Anglo-American heritage, and by the leading members of the Western European community.

In approving that statement, the justices agreed that standards of decency are rising in the United States. They agreed that the law should reflect society. Where the people are growing more humane, the law should become more humane.

Justice Sandra Day O'Connor voted with the majority. But she said there should be more study before the Court decided whether the execution of minors is *always* unconstitutional.

The question remained: Below what age should capital punishment be forbidden? In 1989, the Supreme Court took up the question in *Stanford* v. *Kentucky* and *Wilkins* v. *Missouri*. The defendants were sixteen and seventeen years old. The Court supported capital punishment in both cases. In 1990 Dalton Prejean was convicted in Louisiana for murdering a policeman and was sentenced to death. He was seventeen when he committed the crime. Prejean was also black and retarded. However, the Supreme Court allowed the execution. The justices said that he was old enough. They added that he was retarded but not insane, and that he knew right from wrong. They also held that, although he was black, racial discrimination was not involved. They found no reason to set aside the death sentence.

What about the age limit in other countries? Most that are on record have forbidden the execution of minors under sixteen. Amnesty International keeps track of the statistics. It reported that during the period from 1980 to 1990 only five nations executed juvenile criminals. They were Bangladesh, Barbados, Iran, Iraq, and the United States.

Unfair sentences are a real problem for American justice. They come in many forms. The victims may be members of minority groups that are disliked by other groups. The victims may hold political opinions that are unpopular. An individual may face a prejudiced court because of his or her appearance. A man who comes into court unshaven, with long hair, and dressed in rumpled clothing may not be treated as fairly as a man who is neat and well dressed. Convicted criminals may spend so much time on death row that critics say it is unfair to carry out a death sentence. The danger of unfair, cruel, and unusual sentences exists wherever prejudiced juries can vote in a prejudiced manner. The Eighth Amendment is a shield against such violations of justice.

CHAPTER 8

The Insanity Plea

"How amazing it is that, in the midst of controversies on every conceivable subject, one should expect unanimity of opinion upon difficult legal questions!"

CHIEF JUSTICE CHARLES EVANS HUGHES,
in a speech to the American Law Institute, 1936

Should men and women who are out of their minds be put to death for committing murder? It might seem easy to answer obviously not; to do so would be cruel and unusual punishment, and therefore barred by the Eighth Amendment. But the legal answer is not so simple. The phrase "out of their minds" has many meanings. It has been applied to people who are merely odd as well as to the completely deranged. As a result, the insanity plea is difficult to handle. Many murderers have escaped execution because their lawyers persuaded judges and juries to consider them not responsible for their actions.

Are the Insane Responsible?

The term *insanity* has legal as well as medical definitions. To be legally insane means to have a mental illness to such a degree that

President James A. Garfield was shot by Charles J. Guiteau in 1881. The president lay near death for eighty days, during which time bulletins such as these were displayed in New York City. At Guiteau's trial, the accused acted abnormally. His lawyer claimed Guiteau was not responsible for his acts because of insanity. The jury convicted Guiteau, who was sentenced to death and hanged.

one is not legally responsible for one's acts. How are courts to determine criminal responsibility? What if a defendant claims that he or she was insane at the time of a crime?

One definition has been provided by the American Law Institute in its Model Penal Code. Some states and many federal courts have adopted it, sometimes after making slight changes:

> A person is not responsible for criminal conduct if at the time of such conduct as a result of mental disease or defect he lacks substantial capacity either to appreciate the criminality (wrongfulness) of his conduct or to conform his conduct to the requirements of law.

In some states, once the insanity plea is made by the defense, it is up to the prosecution to prove that the defendant is mentally well. In other states, it is up to the defense to prove that the defendant is insane. In federal criminal cases, the lawyers for the defendant have to prove the defendant's insanity by clear and convincing evidence.

The *Leopold-Loeb* case in Chicago in 1924 is the United States's most famous example of the insanity plea. Clarence Darrow, the defense lawyer in the *Leopold-Loeb* case, made a name for himself when he used the insanity plea to save his clients from execution.

Richard Loeb, seventeen, and Nathan Leopold, Jr., eighteen, were the "thrill killers" of Chicago. They kidnapped a boy named Bobby Franks and brutally murdered him. When they were caught, it seemed that the path before them led through the court directly to the gallows and death by hanging.

Clarence Darrow opposed the death penalty for any criminals, and he was determined to get around it in this case. He used the insanity plea as the weapon with which to defend Leopold and Loeb. True, Darrow made a point of their age, referring to them as "boys" in the hope of persuading the jury to be soft on them. Still, Darrow's real argument was the insanity plea.

The lawyer had to argue skillfully because Leopold and Loeb were not obviously insane. They had coolly plotted the crime, carried it out step-by-step, and tried to cover their tracks with false clues. Didn't so much careful planning prove they were sane when they committed the crime? Darrow thought not. He said in his address to the jury: "But we are told they planned. Well, what does that mean? A maniac plans, an idiot plans, an animal plans, any brain that functions may plan. But their plans were the diseased plans of the diseased mind."

Nathan Leopold, Jr., (left) and Richard Loeb at their murder trial in 1924. On the advice of their lawyer, Clarence Darrow, they used the insanity plea. The confessed killers received sentences of life imprisonment.

Darrow's argument carried the day. Leopold and Loeb received life sentences. A cry went up from the public and the newspapers. The complaint was that the scaffold had been cheated. Condemnations of the insanity plea became numerous.

Rules for the Insane

The *Leopold-Loeb* case is important because of doubts that the defendants were really insane. Lawyers and crime experts said that the M'Naghten Rule of Britain should have been followed. Then Loeb and Leopold would have been found sane enough to be executed.

The M'Naghten Rule is named for Daniel M'Naghten (pronounced muk-NOT-un), who shot and killed the prime minister's secretary in London in 1843. M'Naghten suffered from delusions. He believed he was being persecuted. A psychiatrist who examined him testified that "he was afraid of going out after dark for fear of assassination." The British court considered the following questions. When M'Naghten committed the crime, did he understand what he was doing? Did he know right from wrong? No, to both questions, said the judge. The defendant went to the insane asylum instead of to the gallows.

The M'Naghten Rule is used in several states as a test for the defense of insanity. Under the M'Naghten Rule, an accused person is not criminally responsible if the following things can be proved.

- First, if at the time of committing the crime, the accused was suffering from a disease of the mind so as not to know the nature and quality of the act he or she was doing.
- Second, if the accused did know what he or she was doing, he or she did not at the time of the act know that the act was wrong and a violation of the rights of others.

American politics produced an insanity plea more than forty years before the *Leopold-Loeb* case. In 1881 Charles J. Guiteau shot and killed President James A. Garfield in the Washington, D.C., railroad station. Guiteau was a disappointed office seeker who blamed the president for his failure to get a job in government service. His mental abnormalities gave his lawyer the chance to introduce an insanity plea. The court atmosphere made the plea unsuccessful. The defendant had murdered the president. The M'Naghten Rule was ignored. Guiteau received a death sentence. Historians have called his execution unjust because of his disturbed mental condition.

A more recent insanity plea that gained worldwide attention was that of John W. Hinckley, Jr., in 1981. Hinckley fired shots at President Ronald Reagan and his aides. The president was wounded but recovered fully. But one of his party, James Brady, suffered permanent brain damage. News cameras caught much of the scene. Viewers who saw the attack on their television screens were horrified. Hinckley later received a verdict of not guilty by reason of insanity.

Special Problems

During the 1980s, the Supreme Court looked at some special problems of the insanity plea. In *Ford* v. *Wainwright* (1986), the Supreme Court declared that sane murderers could not be executed if they went insane on death row. Nevertheless, they could be executed if they regained their sanity.

Multiple personality makes possible an unusual type of not-guilty plea—not guilty because the personality on trial is not the personality who committed the crime. The problem reached a Florida court in 1979, when Juanita Maxwell was acquitted of murder. Maxwell had contended that she had seven personalities inhabiting her body and that the crime was committed by her

Police officers and Secret Service agents immediately after John W. Hinckley, Jr., attempted to kill President Ronald Reagan in 1981. Hinckley received a verdict of not guilty by reason of insanity for his attempt at assassination.

personality named Wanda. Juanita claimed she could not be held responsible for what Wanda did. The court accepted the plea. Then Juanita was back in court in 1990, claiming that Wanda committed bank robberies of which Juanita was accused.

The puzzles of insanity and multiple personality have created a situation filled with doubts and contradictions. It is bad enough that ordinary people differ about who is responsible and who is not. But professionals also differ. Whenever there is an insanity plea, there is usually a psychiatrist in court on each side—one supporting the insanity plea, the other rejecting it. Consequently, no single formula covers applications of the Eighth Amendment's protection against cruel and unusual punishments to mental problems. Psychiatry offers no fool-proof barrier to the imposition of cruel and unusual punishments when the insanity plea is before the court.

Will a nearly sane murderer go to the insane asylum rather than to the gas chamber? Will a demented murderer go to the gas chamber rather than to the insane asylum? Both of these possibilities remain open only too often under present conditions.

CHAPTER 9

Should the Death Penalty Be Abolished?

"Excessive bail shall not be required, nor excessive fines imposed, nor cruel and unusual punishments inflicted."

THE EIGHTH AMENDMENT, 1791

The title of this chapter is a question that all those concerned about the Eighth Amendment must consider. If you think the death penalty is cruel and unusual punishment, then you probably want to see an end to it. If you think it is not cruel and unusual, then you probably favor keeping it. Or you may take a position in between and say the death penalty should be abolished except for special cases. For example, Israel keeps the death penalty only for Nazi war criminals.

There are strong arguments for these positions. Many of them have been argued before the Supreme Court.

The Basic Question

Let us look at the basic arguments YES and NO in considering the question, Should the death penalty be abolished? Imagine that two partisans are speaking vehemently to one another.

The Eighth Amendment plays an important part in the American system of justice. Controversies over it continue as courts set bail and impose fines and other punishments. Debate over the death penalty's usefulness and morality continue.

YES. The death penalty is a violation of the human dignity of the criminal.

NO. The death penalty is a defense of the human dignity of the victim.

YES. Innocent persons have been found guilty and wrongly put to death.

NO. Innocent persons have been saved from becoming more victims of executed criminals.

YES. Execution is a horrible act, and no method used can make it humane.

NO. Murder is a horrible act and is frequently more inhumane than any execution.

YES. The death penalty is revenge in which the state makes the criminal pay "an eye for an eye."

NO. The death penalty is retribution in which the state makes the punishment fit the crime.

YES. Murderers who are not executed have a chance to be reformed and turned into responsible citizens.

NO. Murderers who are not executed have a chance to gain their freedom and commit more crimes.

YES. The death penalty is cruel and should follow the rack and the stake into the list of discarded cruel punishments.

NO. The death penalty should be kept as a unique punishment for a unique crime, murder.

YES. Execution does not deter, which is proven by murder statistics.

NO. Execution does deter, for common sense tells us that some people avoid murder for fear of the death penalty.

YES. The death penalty has historically been imposed unfairly against particular groups. For example, statistics support evidence of discrimination against African-American men.

NO. Enforcement of recent laws and court rulings eliminates bias and lead to fair sentencing, including the death penalty where appropriate.

In 1949 Lord Justice Denning testified before Britain's Royal Commission on Capital Punishment. He defended the death penalty: "The truth is that some crimes are so outrageous that society insists on adequate punishment, because the wrong-doer deserves it." Yet, in 1965 Britain abolished the death penalty.

Throughout most of the world, opinion has been against capital punishment. Most Western democracies and many other countries have abandoned it. True, Ireland and a few other nations still execute criminals. But the trend is unmistakeable. Mexico abolished the death penalty in 1931, Canada in 1976, Norway in 1979, France in 1981, and the Philippines in 1987. Amnesty International declared in 1988 that "there is no place in civilized society for the gas chamber, the gallows, or the electric chair."

The American League to Abolish Capital Punishment has not succeeded in persuading the United States to accept its point of view. Recent polls have shown that about 75 percent of Americans support capital punishment. The Supreme Court has consistently taken the position that the death penalty is constitutional. The Court has said that when the rights of the condemned are fully protected and trials have been fair, then the death penalty is not cruel and unusual. Still, some justices have strongly opposed capital punishment in all cases. Here are two different opinions expressed by members of the Supreme Court, the first *for* the death penalty, the second *against* it.

Justice Byron R. White wrote the following in his opinion in *Furman* v. *Georgia* (1972): "It is perhaps true that no matter how infrequently those convicted of rape or murder are executed, the penalty so imposed is not disproportionate to the crime and those executed may deserve exactly what they received."

Justice Thurgood Marshall wrote the following in his dissenting opinion in *Gregg* v. *Georgia* (1976): "The death penalty, unnecessary to promote the goal of deterrence or to further any legitimate notion of retribution, is an excessive penalty forbidden by the Eighth and Fourteen Amendments." There is no easy solution.

The Eighth Amendment

The Eighth Amendment is fundamental to American democracy because it protects those who get into trouble with the law. It protects their rights when they are dealt with by the courts. Has the guilt or innocence of the accused not yet been decided? Bail may be required, but it cannot be too high. Has the accused been found guilty and fined? The fine cannot be too high. If the accused is sentenced to other punishment, it cannot be cruel or unusual. What about capital punishment? Even here there are safeguards to keep the condemned from unnecessary suffering. Whatever the charges, the Eighth Amendment is there to protect all defendants.

IMPORTANT DATES

1215 Magna Carta is signed by King John of England.

1689 English Bill of Rights is accepted by William and Mary.

1776 Virginia Declaration of Rights is adopted.

1776 Declaration of Independence is signed.

1787 Congress passes the Northwest Ordinance.

1788 U.S. Constitution is ratified by most states.

1791 Bill of Rights is ratified by the states.

1833 U.S. Supreme Court decides the case of *Barron* v. *Baltimore*. Says that Bill of Rights does not apply to the states.

1843 M'Naghten Rule on insanity pleas is developed in England.

1868 Fourteenth Amendment is ratified by the states. States cannot deny the "privileges or immunities" of its citizens or take away "life, liberty, or property, without due process of law."

1887 Four of the 1886 Haymarket Riot convicted radicals are executed.

1910 U.S. Supreme Court in *Weems* v. *United States* rules that it is cruel and unusual punishment to hold for twelve to twenty years at hard and painful labor a person convicted of helping to make a false statement on a public document.

1924 Clarence Darrow with an insanity plea saves Leopold and Loeb from the death penalty.

1927 Sacco and Vanzetti are executed.

1951 U.S. Supreme Court in *Stack* v. *Boyle* offers some guidelines for judges about what is excessive bail.

1958 U.S. Supreme Court in *Trop* v. *Dulles* holds that it is cruel and unusual punishment for a person convicted of wartime military desertion to lose his citizenship.

1961 Manhattan Bail project founded.

1962 U.S. Supreme Court in *Robinson* v. *California* rules that it is cruel and unusual punishment to put in prison for up to ninety days a person because he is addicted to the use of narcotics. The right to protection against cruel and unusual punishment is incorporated and so protects citizens against actions by the states.

1966 Congress passes the Bail Reform Act of 1966, which says that for noncapital crimes, under most circumstances, bail cannot be denied.

1968 U.S. Supreme Court in *Witherspoon* v. *Illinois* rules that jurors who are hesitant about, but not absolutely opposed to, capital punishment may serve on juries in cases that might lead to the death penalty.

1972 U.S. Supreme Court in *Furman* v. *Georgia* rules that the death penalty, as then imposed by the states, is cruel and unusual punishment and therefore unconstitutional.

1976 U.S. Supreme Court in *Gregg* v. *Georgia* rules that the death penalty is constitutional if it is decided upon in a consistent and reasonable way, if the sentencing follows strict guidelines, and if the penalty is not required for certain crimes.

1976 U.S. Supreme Court in *Roberts* v. *Louisiana I* rules that mandatory death penalty laws that require the death penalty for every defendant convicted of murder are unconstitutional.

1977 U.S. Supreme Court in *Coker* v. *Georgia* rules that the death penalty is unconstitutional for rape of an adult woman that did not result in her death.

1983 U.S. Supreme Court in *Solem* v. *Helm* rules that it was cruel and unusual punishment to impose a life sentence without possibility of parole on a person convicted of a number of nonviolent crimes including writing a bad check. Court provides guidelines for considering what is a proportionate punishment.

1984 Congress passes the Bail Reform Act of 1984, which withdrew the right to bail for all crimes not punishable by death, gave judges freedom to deny bail to defendants who might become a danger to society, and set guidelines for those to be set free on bail.

1986 U.S. Supreme Court in *Lockhart* v. *McCree* rules that those absolutely opposed to the death penalty can be kept from serving on juries that decide both the guilt and the sentencing in cases that could involve the death penalty.

1987 U.S. Supreme Court in *United States* v. *Salerno* rules that defendants can be denied bail if they might be a danger to society.

1988 U.S. Supreme Court in *Thompson* v. *Oklahoma* overturns the death penalty of a convicted murderer who had been fifteen at the time of the murder.

GLOSSARY

aggravating circumstances   Facts or events surrounding a crime that would make it appear worse. Aggravating circumstances may be used to increase the sentence for a crime.

amendment   A change in the Constitution.

appeal   To refer a case to a higher court so that it will review the decision of a lower court.

arraignment   A process in which the accused person is brought before a court to plead to the criminal charge against him or her. The accused person is asked to plead guilty or not guilty.

bail   Money paid by the accused to gain his or her release in the period before trial to make sure he or she will show up for the trial. If the accused does not appear, he or she loses the money.

bill of attainder   A law pronouncing a person guilty of a serious crime without a trial.

capital crime   A very serious crime in which the accused can be given the death sentence if he or she is found guilty.

civil case   A law case in which private individuals or businesses sue each other over property or money.

common law   Law based not on acts passed by lawmaking bodies but rather on customs, traditions, and court decisions.

concurring opinion   An opinion by one or more judges that agrees with the majority opinion but offers different reasons for reaching the decision.

counsel   A lawyer who may appear on behalf of a person in civil or criminal trials or other legal proceedings.

criminal case   A law case involving a crime against society (such as robbery or murder), punished by the government.

defendant   The accused person, who must defend himself or herself against a formal charge. In criminal cases, this means the person officially accused of a crime.

dissenting opinion   An opinion by one or more of a court's judges that disagrees with a majority opinion.

executive branch   The branch or part of the government that carries out the laws and makes sure they are obeyed.

ex post facto **law**   A law that makes illegal an action that took place before the law was passed.

federalism   The system by which the states and the federal government each have certain special powers and share others.

fine   A money payment that a person convicted of an offense is required to pay.

habeas corpus   The right of someone who has been arrested to be brought into court and formally charged.

incorporation   The process of making Bill of Rights protections apply to the states so that people are safeguarded against state actions violating these rights.

indictment   A grand jury's written accusation that the person named has committed a crime.

information   A written accusation presented not by a grand jury but by a public prosecutor, charging a person with a crime.

insanity   As legally defined, a condition of having a mental disease to such a degree that a person is not legally responsible for his or her act.

judicial activism   A trend among courts or judges to expand their powers by making policy.

judicial branch   The part or branch of the government that interprets the laws.

judicial restraint   The belief that judges should have great respect for legislatures and executives, overruling their actions only when such actions are clearly unconstitutional.

judicial review   The power of the courts to review the decisions of other parts or levels of the government. A court may review the decision of a lower court and come to a different decision.

legislative branch   The part or branch of the government that makes the laws.

M'Naghten Rule   Guidelines developed in England in 1843 by which one can determine if an accused person is criminally responsible.

majority opinion   The statement of a court's decision in which the majority of its members join.

mitigating circumstances   Facts or events surrounding a crime that, while not an excuse for the crime, may be considered in fairness and mercy as reducing the amount of blame. Mitigating circumstances may be used to lessen the sentence for a crime.

parole   Release from prison after actually serving part of the sentence. The criminal is released from prison on condition that he or she follows the rules outlined in the parole order.

precedent   A previous decision of a court that is used as an example or powerful reason for a same or similar decision in a new case that is similar in facts or legal principles.

pretrial detention   The holding of a defendant in a criminal case in a prison or other place before his or her trial. The person is held because of fears the person might flee before the trial or might be of harm to the community.

probation A sentence imposed for a crime whereby a convicted criminal is released under the supervision of a probation officer instead of being in prison. The defendant must behave well—or he or she will go to prison.

public prosecutor A lawyer who works for the government (such as a state's attorney or district attorney) and who tries to prove that the accused person is guilty of the crime charged.

ratification Approval of an amendment to the Constitution by three-fourths of state legislatures or conventions (after the amendment has been officially proposed by two-thirds of each house of Congress or proposed by a convention called by two-thirds of the states).

recidivist A criminal who repeatedly commits crimes.

separation of powers The division of the government into three parts or branches—the legislative, the executive, and the judicial.

subpoena A legal order for a person to appear in court and testify.

suspect A person believed to be involved in a crime.

testify In a legal proceeding such as a trial, to give evidence after taking an oath or affirmation.

verdict The official decision of a jury.

warrant A written document issued by a government official that gives an officer the power to carry out an arrest, search, seizure, or other action.

witness A person whose statements under oath are received as evidence for any purpose.

writ of assistance A written document issued by a government official allowing an officer to conduct an almost unlimited search and seizure and to ask for help in doing so.

$\mathcal{S}$UGGESTED $\mathcal{R}$EADING

*Adler, Mortimer. *We Hold These Truths: Understanding the Ideas and Ideals of the Constitution.* New York: Macmillan, 1987.

Amnesty International. *The Death Penalty.* London: Amnesty International Publications, 1979.

Bedau, Hugo Adam, ed. *The Death Penalty in America.* New York: Oxford University Press. 3rd ed., 1982.

The Bill of Rights and Beyond: A Resource Guide. The Commission on the Bicentennial of the United States Constitution, 1990.

Brant, Irving. *The Bill of Rights: Its Origins and Meaning.* Indianapolis, Ind.: Bobbs-Merrill, 1965.

Clark, Ramsey. *Crime in America.* New York: Simon and Schuster, 1970.

Conrad, John P., and Ernest van den Haag. *The Death Penalty: A Debate.* New York: Plenum, 1983.

*Davis, Bertha. *Instead of Prison.* New York: Franklin Watts, 1986.

Hood, Roger. *The Death Penalty: A World-Wide Perspective.* New York: Oxford University Press, 1989.

*Kohn, Bernice. *The Struggle for Rights in America.* New York: Viking, 1974.

Levy, Leonard W., Kenneth L. Karst, and Denis J. Mahoney, eds. *Encyclopedia of the American Constitution.* New York: Macmillan, 1986.

McCafferty, James A., ed. *Capital Punishment.* Chicago: Aldine-Atherton, 1972.

*Miers, Earl Schenck. *The Bill of Rights.* New York: Grosset and Dunlap, 1968.

Rutland, Robert A. *The Birth of the Bill of Rights, 1776–1791.* Chapel Hill: University of North Carolina Press, 1955.

*Schwartz, Bernard. *American Heritage History of the Law in America.* New York: American Heritage, 1974.

Woodward, Bob, and Scott Armstrong. *The Brethren: Inside the Supreme Court.* New York: Simon and Schuster, 1979.

*Readers of *The Eighth Amendment* by Vincent Buranelli may find this book particularly readable.

$\mathscr{S}$OURCES

Adler, Mortimer. *We Hold These Truths: Understanding the Ideas and Ideals of the Constitution.* New York: Macmillan, 1987.

Amnesty International. *The Death Penalty.* London: Amnesty International Publications, 1979.

Bedau, Hugo Adam, ed. *The Death Penalty in America.* New York: Oxford University Press. 3rd ed., 1982.

Bork, Robert H. *The Tempting of America: The Political Seduction of the Law.* New York: Free Press, 1990.

Brant, Irving. *The Bill of Rights: Its Origins and Meaning.* Indianapolis: Bobbs-Merrill, 1965.

Brant, Irving. *James Madison: Father of the Constitution, 1787–1800.* Indianapolis: Bobbs-Merrill, 1950.

Clark, Ramsey. *Crime in America.* New York: Simon and Schuster, 1970.

Conrad, John P., and Ernest van den Haag. *The Death Penalty: A Debate.* New York: Plenum, 1983.

Corwin, Edward S. *The Constitution and What It Means Today.* Revised by Harold W. Chase and Craig R. Ducat. Princeton: Princeton University Press, 1978.

Davis, Bertha. *Instead of Prison.* New York: Franklin Watts, 1986.

Douglas, William O. *A Living Bill of Rights.* New York: Doubleday, 1961.

Flemming, Roy B. *Punishment Before Trial: An Organizational Perspective on Felony Bail Processes.* New York and London: Longman, 1982.

Freed, Daniel J., and Patricia M. Wald. *Bail in the United States.* Washington, D.C.: U.S. Department of Justice, 1964.

Goldkamp, John S. *Two Classes of Accused: A Study of Bail Detention in American Justice.* Cambridge, Mass.: Ballinger, 1979.

Gooderson, R. N. "Diminished Responsibility. The McNaghten Rules." *The Oxford Companion to the Mind.* New York: Oxford University Press, 1987, pp. 193–195.

Hood, Roger. *The Death Penalty: A World-Wide Perspective.* New York: Oxford University Press, 1989.

Kohn, Bernice. *The Struggle for Rights in America.* New York: Viking, 1974.

Levy, Leonard W., Kenneth L. Karst, and Denis J. Mahoney, eds. *Encyclopedia of the American Constitution.* New York: Macmillan, 1986.

Loeb, Robert H., Jr. *Crime and Punishment.* New York: Franklin Watts, 1985.

McCafferty, James A., ed. *Capital Punishment.* Chicago: Aldine-Atherton, 1972.

Maeder, Thomas. *Crime and Madness: The Origins and Evolution of the Insanity Defense.* New York: Harper and Row, 1985.

Miers, Earl Schenck. *The Bill of Rights.* New York: Grosset and Dunlap, 1968.

Padover, Saul K. *The Living U.S. Constitution.* 2nd rev. ed. by Jacob W. Landynski. New York: New American Library, 1983.

Radelet, Michael L., ed. *Facing the Death Penalty: Essays on a Cruel and Unusual Punishment.* Philadelphia: Temple University Press, 1989.

Royal Commission on Capital Punishment. *Report.* London: Her Majesty's Stationery Office, 1953.

Rutland, Robert A. *The Birth of the Bill of Rights, 1776–1791.* Chapel Hill: University of North Carolina Press, 1955.

Rutland, Robert A. *George Mason: Reluctant Statesman.* Williamsburg, Va.: Colonial Williamsburg, 1961.

Schwartz, Bernard. *American Heritage History of the Law in America.* New York: American Heritage, 1974.

Sheleff, Leon S. *Ultimate Penalties: Capital Punishment, Life Imprisonment, Torture.* Columbus: Ohio State University Press, 1987.

Siegel, Mark, and Nancy R. Jacobs, eds. *Capital Punishment: Cruel and Unusual?* Plano, Texas: Instructional Aids, 1982.

Simon, Rita J. *The Jury and the Defense of Insanity.* Boston: Little, Brown, 1967.

State Courts and Law-Related Education. Bethesda, Md.: Phi Alpha Delta Public Service Center, 1985.

Streib, Victor L. *The Death Penalty for Juveniles.* Bloomington: Indiana University Press, 1987.

Thomas, Wayne H., Jr. *Bail Reform in America.* Berkeley: University of California Press, 1976.

West, Donald, and Alexander Walk, eds. *Daniel McNaghten: His Trial and the Aftermath.* London: Gaskell Books, 1977.

Woodward, Bob, and Scott Armstrong. *The Brethren: Inside the Supreme Court.* New York: Simon and Schuster, 1979.

INDEX OF CASES

Author's Acknowledgments

The author wishes to thank librarian Anne Jones and her staff at the Shepard-Pruden Memorial Library in Edenton, North Carolina, for their help in obtaining books without which this one could not have been written.

Vincent Buranelli is the author of eleven books and numerous articles in history and biography. He has previously written for American Heritage and Silver Burdett Press, including a biography of Thomas A. Edison for Silver Burdett Press's *Pioneers in Change* series. Buranelli holds an M.A. in political science from the National University of Ireland and a Ph.D. from Cambridge University.

Vincent Buranelli's first book identified James Alexander as the guiding spirit behind Peter Zenger's newspaper, which started freedom of the press in colonial New York. He and his wife collaborated on an encyclopedia of espionage. Buranelli is now working on a biography of Robert Louis Stevenson. He lives in Edenton, North Carolina, and is a member of the Authors Guild.

Warren E. Burger was Chief Justice of the United States from 1969 to 1986. Since 1985 he has served as chairman of the Commission on the Bicentennial of the United States Constitution. He is also chancellor of the College of William and Mary, Williamsburg, Virginia; chancellor emeritus of the Smithsonian Institution; and a life trustee of the National Geographic Society. Prior to his appointment to the Supreme Court, Chief Justice Burger was Assistant Attorney General of the United States (Civil Division) and judge of the United States Court of Appeals, District of Columbia Circuit.

Philip A. Klinkner graduated from Lake Forest College in 1985 and is now finishing his Ph.D. in political science at Yale University. He is currently a Governmental Studies Fellow at the Brookings Institution in Washington, D.C. Klinkner is the author of *The First Amendment* and *The Ninth Amendment* in *The American Heritage History of the Bill of Rights*.